EMMANUEL IN ALL MY MOMENTS

EMMANUEL IN ALL MY MOMENTS

ANNIE ELIZABETH SNYDER

CONTENTS

Jesus – my Savior, my Redeemer, my Healer, my Friend.
This is for you. You get the glory. All of the glory

Unless otherwise indicated, scripture quotations are from the ESV® Bible (The Holy Bible, English Standard Version®), © 2001 by Crossway, a publishing ministry of Good News Publishers. Used by permission. All rights reserved.

Scripture quotations marked TPT are from The Passion Translation®. Copyright © 2017, 2018, 2020 by Passion & Fire Ministries, Inc. Used by permission. All rights reserved. ThePassionTranslation.com.

ISBN: 979-8-9994151-1-0

Published by One Thing I Ask Publishing
Cover design by: Annie Elizabeth Snyder
First Edition 2025 / Printed in the United States of America

Here's what I've learned through it all: don't give up; don't be impatient; be entwined as one with the Lord. Be brave and courageous, and never lose hope. Yes, keep on waiting — for he will never disappoint you!

Psalm 27:14 TPT

Because you are close to me and always available, my confidence will never be shaken, for I experience your wrap-around presence every moment.

Psalm 16:8 TPT

CONTENT WARNING

This book contains sensitive content, including discussions of eating disorders, self-harm, suicide, and sexual abuse. These topics are mentioned to emphasize that nobody is alone in their struggles. We have a God who is with us in the midst of it all. Despite these difficult themes, hope has not been forgotten. It has been found. A living hope. And I live to tell my story of God redeeming and restoring years I thought were lost and stolen. Revelation 19:10 states, "For the testimony of Jesus is the spirit of prophecy." What He has done for one, He can do for another. May you find hope and healing within the pages of this book.

MY VISION

My prayer has been that people will be led to their Healer while reading this. That people will not only feel less alone but have confidence that they are not, and never have been, alone — Emmanuel in every moment. I've designed most chapters to be standalone in the sense that you can pick up the book and simply read any chapter independently. That you can grab hold of a chapter that really encourages you and revisit it. Some chapters are shorter than others. All chapters tell a story of how much we can't do this journey alone and how we need a Savior. This is a story of God being in all of my moments, whether I recognized Him at the time or not. Be encouraged as you read through or skip through these pages. I pray you find hope, healing, and freedom that can only be found in our God — forever Emmanuel.

.

Introduction

It was August 2014. All of my friends were starting at their college of choice this year, but I was not. I was being admitted to the hospital on a hot Sunday afternoon after an overdose. This was the beginning of my battle with depression for the next ten years of my life.

Within these pages, a lot of battles will be mentioned. But not one battle has come that my God hasn't been at the center of. I have seen some of the darkest nights, and still, my God was with me. Recognizing His presence changes everything, and His presence has been woven throughout all the pages of my story. Whether you doubt that a good God can be present when bad things happen or simply doubt that He is a present, living God today, listen to my story. His presence is a golden thread beautifully woven throughout. He is with us every step of the way, in every valley, mountaintop, hospital, and treatment center. I live in the mystery most days that my God was with me in my darkest moments, and yet I thank Him. What a good, kind, faithful, and true God!

So, where do I begin?

I'll share with you some of my background that I took into all of my battles. I grew up in a loving family with three siblings and both of my parents. One of my earliest memories is when I was five years old, sitting with my mom on my parents' bed as I accepted Jesus into my life. When my parents would drop me off at school, I was always asked, "What do you take to school with you every day?" and my response would forever be, "A smile on my face and Jesus in my heart." Jesus was always a topic of conversation in our home. Representing Him to a broken world was another. Then, in 2012, my eyes were opened to the Holy Spirit for the first time, which changed everything about my Christian life and relationship with God.

The truth is we live in a dark world. People seek after all the wrong things and find that none of it satisfies.

Thankfully, in the midst of my own story and search for what could only ever satisfy, I always knew my God was there. Somewhere. Even if I couldn't see past the storm. His promise to never leave was known from church growing up and became a reality that I have held fast to for the last decade of my life. Beautiful Emmanuel — God with us.

That hospital visit in 2014 was marked by God making Himself known even in the midst of such pain and darkness. When the doctors told me, "There is nothing in your system," I knew it was God. It could've only been God — a miracle. And then there was my roommate. After being in the ER, they transferred me upstairs to the psychiatric unit. A police officer escorted me in silence as we rode an elevator to the 5th floor. My roommate was a stranger who became like a sister to me. In the midst of her pain, there were moments when I was able to tell her about Jesus and share with her how present God was. Even in her pain, confusion, and hurt, God was closer than any thought she had or the weapon she had been holding onto. My roommate passed away a few years ago, and although I grieve, I also thank God for the conversations I had with her about Jesus.

In the following pages, you will read more of my story. Pain is present, but my God's present even more so. Emmanuel is in these moments.

Equipped

God equips us for the battles that we enter into. Looking back on the last decade of my life, God gave me His promises to hold fast to and to fight with. How wild to think about that. Let me explain more.

God began to show me who He was — forever present, the God who heals, the God who sees, constant in the midst of storms where I would believe otherwise if it weren't for His Truth piercing through.

Throughout every painful memory or event mentioned in this book, my God shows up. He never failed.

His presence has been like a golden thread woven throughout all my pain. Holding together wound upon wound like stitches, carrying healing with every touch. If it weren't for His presence, I would not be writing this book today. I probably wouldn't be alive.

First, He introduced Himself to me as Emmanuel — God with us.

"Be strong and courageous. Do not fear or be in dread of them, for it is the Lord your God who goes with you. He will not leave you or forsake you." Deuteronomy 31:6 (ESV, emphasis added)

"No man shall be able to stand before you all the days of your life. Just as I was with Moses, so I will be with you. I will not leave you or forsake you." Joshua 1:5 (ESV, emphasis added)
"Even though I walk through the valley of the shadow of death,
I will fear no evil,
for you are with me;
your rod and your staff,
they comfort me." Psalm 23:4 (ESV, emphasis added)
"And I will ask the Father, and he will give you another Helper, to be with you forever, 17 even the Spirit of truth, whom the world cannot receive, because it neither sees him nor knows him. You know him, for he dwells with you and will be in you." John 14:16-17 (ESV, emphasis added)
"teaching them to observe all that I have commanded you. And behold, I am with you always, to the end of the age." Matt 28:20 (ESV, emphasis added)

God was with me. God dwelled within me.

This filled me with wonder in my sophomore year of high school. To know that the Holy Spirit was present, always. To know that He loves to reveal Himself to us in tangible ways. To know that He still gives gifts and is closer than my very thoughts. I would sit in awe back in high school. I knew God was with me.

I soon began to tread water. The water got deeper, choppier, and colder. The sky got darker, the thunder got louder, and the lightning became brighter. I became more exhausted. I cried out for help, but nobody heard me. His presence was always there. I would sit on the bathroom floor. Suicidal. Just me, a blade in my hand, and pills on my mind. His presence was always there. Did I always recognize it? No. But when I did, it changed everything.

Years later, a random stranger gave me a prophetic word and told me that the Lord saw me on the floor of that bathroom. It was all the reassurance I needed to know that He saw me and knew the pain I was going through. Even on the nights when I felt alone, I was never alone.

Jehovah Rapha — my God revealed Himself as healer right before I began to feel chronic pain in my body. He introduced Himself as healer before I was diagnosed with fibromyalgia. How intentional. I would never look at it as God dangling before me a promise that He had for some and not for me. I felt the Lord giving that promise to me to hold fast to in the middle of the fire, heat, sharp shooting pain, and aches. Jehovah Rapha. "I am your healer, Annie. The sun of righteousness will rise with healing in its wings. There is healing in My wings, Annie. Reach out like the woman in Luke 8 and touch the hem of My garment. I know your arms are weak and exhausted, but I will meet you in your weakness." I also experienced God as Jehovah Rapha through and through as I walked through forgiveness, which is detailed in another chapter.

El Roi — my God introduced Himself to me as the God who sees right before traumatic memories started coming back to the surface. If it weren't known that God saw all, I simply don't know what I would've done. Knowing that God saw me, He saw all that was done to me, and He saw all that I was remembering was reassuring. It didn't take away all of the pain and confusion I had, but it helped me to know He was with me in it. He understood.

And throughout all three of my God's names I hold close, He also showed me He is a God of the details. Sprinkled throughout my story — whether in the victories or the struggles — I saw my God showing up in the littlest details. A God so vast and magnificent showed up in my little life, revealing to me that He holds even the tiniest details of my life in His hands — intentionally, purposefully.

That is my story. Finding God deep in the pain and deep in His goodness and faithfulness.

Seen and Safe

Something I believed for years was that if people stared at me, especially men, I wasn't safe. That lie was rooted in the events that took place beginning in middle school with a friend's father. I was sexually abused, and in one moment, I no longer felt safe when I was seen. I felt exposed. I felt seen and unsafe during the day as well as while I was sleeping.

Beginning in sixth grade, I started at a new private school about twenty-five minutes from my house. The school felt safe compared to the one I had just come from. Maybe what made it feel safe was a fresh start. It was a new beginning. Compared to the other school, nobody had done harm to me. I hadn't been bullied. It would be a new beginning, I thought, every family desiring a classical Christian education. We would sing hymns in the morning, we would pray, and there was grace given by teachers. My mom was a teacher there herself, and I would often get there early before the halls were filled with students. I remember the quiet that filled the stairwells before and after school. But starting at this new school, I had no idea I would soon become a target. Not by students, teachers, or the public but by a parent. A friend's father. The nightmare would quickly unfold. Being the new girl set me up. Entering my seventh-grade year, I became friends with someone. Innocent, fun, and what I thought was normal. Looking back, none of it was normal. None of it was okay. I always remember being greeted by the whole family whenever I'd come over. Greeted with hugs and backed by so much control that I was simply blind to. It was an innocent time until her father sexually abused me.

That is the first memory I have of pure, paralyzing fear that gripped my body and took my breath away. I still remember the feeling and where I was. Stuck. Frozen. Unable to physically move in the middle of the night. I lay on my left side, waiting for him to leave the room. I don't remember the rest of the night or the next morning.

But our minds protect us, and I repressed those memories throughout our friendship. I was blinded by the extravagance of all we did and all we were treated to. We went to countless concerts, all of which, of course, were VIP. The first year I met this girl, I was also invited to go on an international trip with them for spring break. That friendship included a lot of "don't tell your parents" moments and beach trips that never should've taken place. Later on in high school, as I was fundraising for one of my mission trips, I received an extravagant donation signed by the father, the mother, and the daughter. An arms-length, across town, "I can't take back all I did to you, but here's a donation." That friendship included a lot of finding the friend's father just around the corner at any moment. I do remember mentioning to my mom that he was around a lot, but there was nothing else to it that my mind would allow me to remember. I was constantly being watched if I wasn't being touched.

I can easily say that seventh grade was the root of my fear and everything that was to come. I struggled with shame, self-hatred, anxiety, and depression. Fear of men and any man the same age as my abuser. That association ruined relationships for years as I was afraid to interact with anyone who seemed anything like this man simply by age and gender, which included my own dad. People couldn't understand, and what was happening was devastating to me.

Entering into 8th grade, I didn't have a recollection of what he had done, but I thought I had done something. There was a weight of shame that took my voice away. I was scared of authority and, looking back, scared of anyone who would've been on my side and helped me. Shame turned into anxiety, which turned into depression as I looked for ways of escape. Ways out of the mess that I felt I had created. Whatever that mess was. I just couldn't remember.

So, where was God in the middle of it all?

Right there with me.

God is Protector, is He not? God is also El Roi, the God who sees so surely He isn't missing these moments. My Protector is just going to let it happen?

How could something terrible happen in His presence?

We live in a fallen world where man has free will.

But God never left me. I was never alone in that room in the middle of the night — just me and that man. God was there. Emmanuel — beautiful Emmanuel. I got through those horrible nights with Him by my side.

I remember years later, I was living in California and woke up one night to the Lord's whisper saying, "You're precious in my sight." What was significant about this was that He had spoken that right after I woke up from sleeping, being seen while sleeping. But God. His words were like healing honey. In the next few weeks, He began to speak "Seen and Safe. Seen and Safe." One moment of utter darkness was the start of me feeling seen, exposed, and anything but safe. And in one moment, my God brought the healing that I didn't know I needed. I was seen and safe.

The years following those events haven't been easy. In fact, middle school was the start of my struggle with OCD. Anxiety, panic, self-harm, and depression came after. Later, I would be engulfed by PTSD and taken over by an eating disorder. Much of it as a way of coping and coping from what? My mind didn't know at the time.

Since then, I have come to find compassion for little me. There's a lot I can't change, but a lot I could tell seventh-grade Annie or anyone else in this position.

I recently wrote a letter to my younger self.

I have always wanted to write a letter to my younger self at this age but have never had the words. A letter from me to me. Not super complicated, right? Well, I can say that seventh grade marked me and my little world in a way that I wouldn't wish on anyone. One letter wouldn't fit all the correct words that I'd want to say, but it would say something. And something is better than nothing. I have found so much compassion for little me and pray that if you find yourself in a similar situation that you can find compassion and grace for yourself as well.

To seventh-grade Annie,

You are loved. You are seen. You are protected. You will come to know God as El Roi — the God who sees. The One who protects. You'll throw yourself deep into trusting in the mystery of who He says He is despite what you will have experienced in your seventh-grade year and beyond. The unimaginable will happen to you this year. Words I don't want to even write back to you. We live in a fallen world, and people do things that can rattle, break, and crush someone's world in one moment or five. You will come to know fear this year in one split moment in a way you have never known it, but God will be your Protector, forever. Emmanuel, forever. He is good, forever. He will never change in the midst of all of it. Because of this year, you will be marked with a heart for justice. Because of this year, you will become convinced that the God of the universe sees you. How wild is that? Time and time again, people are going to cross your path and convince you that God is El Roi. You will overcome battles in the next decade that make you stronger, not weaker. And even in your weakest moments, you'll meet your greatest strength living within you. You will see God bring beauty from ashes. You will see Him turn bitter things into something sweet. You will hear the Lord's sweet voice speak to you in ways you didn't even know were possible and you'll come to know you have a voice even as people try to silence you. You'll come to know His presence in the midst of the blazing fire.

Junior year, you'll begin to know anxiety and depression in ways you probably wouldn't have known if it weren't for the injustice done against you. The anxiety and depression will wrap themselves around your world until you feel like you're suffocating and living isn't possible.

You will battle with knowing that your life is worth living, and you will struggle to know your worth. You will find your comfort in blades and pills.

But know...know this: you are stronger than you think, braver than you know, and you will get through this. All of those nights spent alone in your room, all of those days on the bathroom floor, all of the hours spent in therapy, you'll get through them all. You'll find your voice that was never meant to be silenced. You have a voice and you will find it again.

You'll live so many years thinking that there is no hope for "tomorrow." You'll believe that a decade of your life has been stolen and all of those years are in ruins, completely hopeless for rebuilding. But you'll come to know the good news that God redeems and restores what is lost and stolen. Our God can bring brilliant beauty from deadly, weighty ashes. Your story will be one of dancing upon injustice and disappointment. Dancing under the reign of your king Jesus, the One who has saved you from it all.

You are seen, you are safe. And in His wings, you will find healing. Don't give up hope. You have a story to tell, seventh-grade Annie. And with your voice, you will tell it. But you're never alone in it, for He is with you always... and He has never left.

To anyone who has ever had a similar experience, I am so sorry. It never should've been like this, but we have a kind God who loves to redeem stories and bring beauty from ashes. I can just see Him taking ashes and using them to write a better, brighter, more beautiful story. Emmanuel is in our moments.

I found a journal from my seventh-grade year months ago. Out of a bin of seventy-seven journals, this was the one I pulled out. What was significant was that I found the journal exactly fourteen years later — to the day — from when we left for the international trip. Both picking up that journal and its timing were heavenly, divine timing.

This journal held a play-by-play of everything I did that week. It doesn't feel like a coincidence that the date came to mind the other day, and I knew it was significant but didn't know why until reading through this very journal. The date at the top stood out as if marked in bold and underlined.

It's a wild thing how something like this can affect someone so many years later. That trip was one of just many "extravagant" things I was treated to, but it was a significant one that marked my story and left a scar. On that trip, we also attended a concert —"VIP," as they always were. In seventh grade, Annie was so excited she got to "play" Joe Jonas' guitar.

Reading this made me sad —seventh grade. So much innocence was stolen. Lasting for years and wondering how it could go on so long, but our minds are wild. There are so many questions I have. And I'm letting myself ask them. But no wondering if it allows me to wander away. Wandering away from God, that is. I'm asking the questions and holding His hand. Hand in hand. Staying close. To the only One I can truly trust. The One that's writing this story out. I'm just letting my hand yield to His right now. He's the one who will finish what He started. The one that promises all things — including this — will work together for good ...even this. Somehow.

As I discovered these journal entries, I'm also just thankful. There's a story that will be told — in His timing — and this book is a part of that. He is in the details of even me discovering these journal entries, as hard as it is.

I vividly remember sitting in the airport in Miami singing songs with my friend exactly fourteen years ago. Waiting to board our plane for the "best vacation ever" — the words I read in my journal — a vacation where I had no access to my phone and spoke to my parents once. My phone was taken from me, but my parents didn't know that. My journal documented the restaurants we ate at, the people we met (hello Jonas Brothers — seventh-grade Annie's dream), and the limos we rode in. And the other things I have started to remember. It can wreak havoc if I let it.

But oh, the story I get to tell! My God is forever with me — that I've been sure of — and more sure than ever before. I see God in the details of how I came across these journal entries...exactly fourteen years later. I didn't even know they existed, and honestly, I don't even know the purpose of this. But God has a story to tell through me... and in time, I am letting Him tell it.

Simply a God of the details. Emmanuel. El Roi. Jehovah Rapha. And as I sit with my journal I remember that my God is good — always has been and always will be, even in the painful memories of this.

2014

I had been reaching out for help for a while — parents, pastors, mentors, and friends. It seemed as if people didn't believe me, but they really just didn't know what was going on. People thought I was manipulative and selfish. I was screaming for help, but I didn't know what I was running from myself. The school I attended for middle school and high school caused me a lot of anxiety beginning my sophomore year of high school.

It felt like I was blindfolded and grabbing for anything that could provide relief. My first escape was from volleyball. It made me anxious when the attention was on me. It made me anxious when I messed up. It made me anxious if there was ever conflict. And my OCD shined bright. I had to bounce the volleyball eleven times before I served — each time. I just had to. I enjoyed playing volleyball; it was practically my life at the time, playing both for school and club, but it was also wrapped in so much anxiety and perfectionism that I needed out. I needed to breathe. Not soon enough, I ended up quitting volleyball. I still swam for the swim team at school, which was a healthy outlet, but I remember beginning to struggle more than most people thought. Quitting volleyball didn't take away my anxiety, and my OCD was still very present. I checked outlets, stoves, doors, and light switches numerous times before leaving the house. I

would walk up the stairs and take one step back if that meant someone in my family was going to be "safe." If I drove somewhere, I usually returned to my car to ensure it was in park. OCD danced around
in my mind, making itself known as if it had been welcomed and was
there to stay.

Nobody at my school knew I had anxiety so debilitating. I hid
it well around others. I mean, I was one of the quieter students but
that was just because I took it all in. Once volleyball was out of my
life, school became my life. I would spend endless hours on home-
work each night. If something should've taken one hour, I would
have spent three hours on it. Messing up felt like the end of the
world. In Rhetoric class, I would always try to go first for an assign-
ment to get things over with. I lived my life with my body and mind
wrapped in anxiety.

Soon enough, that anxiety grew. I couldn't do anything without
being anxious. I couldn't walk the halls at school or say "here" for
attendance in the classroom without overthinking, wanting to hide,
and wishing I could escape from the world.

Escape was no longer just a word in my vocabulary at the end of
high school. By junior year, I was pleading with my parents to let
me leave the school I was at. The anxiety boiled over, and I was unable to handle it anymore. I felt like I was screaming for help, and
my screaming seemed to be silent. "I have no voice," I believed. No
voice. "People don't understand me," I thought. "I'm too complicated." All I knew was I needed out of that school. I didn't know
why, but knew I needed to find the "escape." That's when I became
suicidal. I thought I would be better off not here than to be getting
bad grades at the school I was at. I thought I would be better off not
here than to be surrounded by crowds of people in the hallway when
the bell rang. I thought I was better off not being here than being as
anxious as I was.

By my junior year, I was depressed, suicidal, anxious, and felt utterly alone. And my memories of being abused had not yet come to the surface. Things were only going to get worse.

By some miracle, in the new year, I left that school to be home-schooled. I felt safe.

Nevertheless, I still struggled. I didn't know I had a desire to graduate with a class my senior year until it was stripped from me. I would never go to high school reunions or feel like I was a part of that class anymore. High school was just the start of my battle with depression, suicidal thoughts, attempts, and self-harm. I began to find comfort in a blade meeting my skin. Punishment for me. A release for me. I felt I deserved it. I absolutely hated myself. It was during this time that I couldn't sit at a dinner table and say anything without being corrected. People knew I was struggling, and they thought I was doing this to myself. I don't blame them. Nobody knew why I was struggling so much. Neither did I. My memories were still repressed. I just knew I hated myself, and I knew I didn't want to live.

Back to August of 2014. I was writing letters to my family to say goodbye and, soon enough, being admitted to the hospital on a hot summer day after an overdose. The time spent in the ER was necessary but I also had some of the most traumatizing encounters I have had with nurses at the hospital. It was so bad that although I was ashamed of the place I was in, I asked my mom to spend the night with me. She sat in a chair, and I slept in a rock-hard twin bed that wasn't long enough for my legs that night. Maybe treating me like a human would begin if my mom was around, I thought. The next day, I was escorted up by police to the 5th floor. I remember being so scared as I watched my mom leave those closing doors. What had I gotten myself into?

The same day, my roommate came. We became friends fast. We had shared stories of how we had gotten to that very moment of being together...looking out the windows and seeing people come in and out of the hospital...playing with the beds that raised and lowered. When a nurse would come to check on us, one of our beds would be completely raised and one would be as low to the ground as it could go. At the time, the doctors suspected I had an eating disorder when I really just didn't like the hospital food. An eating disorder was not yet a struggle. But I kept snacks in my room, and every time a nurse would come to check on us, my roommate would tell me, and I would begin eating the goldfish crackers. All so that they could see me eating. The memories I have with my roommate sitting across the room from her, telling her about Jesus, are memories I will cherish forever. She told me that she didn't know how she was still alive. I told her that God intervened for a reason. There was a reason she was there with me in the room that day. A few years ago, she passed away, and I will always be thankful for our conversations and the fun we had while it had also been such a dark week for both of us.

That week passed, and I remember as soon as I left the hospital, I went to a country concert. It was as if nothing had just taken place, and nobody knew where I had been for the last week. I lived a secret — not intentionally — that I was struggling and winning the most intense battle with depression anyone could think up. The battle continued, the depression ran wild, and I couldn't find any will to live.

During that season, I remember having to call my therapist while driving on specific roads just to be distracted so I wouldn't run off the road. I remember car rides with my mom where I would be so close to jumping out of the car. My mind wasn't sound. I lived in chaos, and I became used to it. Peels of thunder were white noise in my life. Even still, Emmanuel was present in each moment.

2016

At the end of 2015, I was working with a therapist at Duke. She saw a need for me to get more treatment than I was currently receiving. After doing research, my parents and I decided on a treatment center in Atlanta, Georgia. I remember arriving in the main office, looking around, and wondering how I ended up there — it was the first of February in 2016.

I clung to one Psalm during my time in treatment there. I had written Psalm 91 in the palm of my hand as a reminder that the Lord is my refuge. In my first session with my therapist, she acknowledged the Psalm and I knew I was exactly where I was supposed to be. Although the circumstances weren't great, my God was with me and showing Himself in the smallest details. My therapist would send emails telling me that she was covering me in prayer throughout the day. The littlest things meant the world to me.

I still remember my first day of residential treatment like it was yesterday. They handed me the key to my room and I headed upstairs. Alone. Stepping on the carpet softly trying not to make a sound for the guys that lived below me. I barely put my bags down before I started having a mild panic attack. I didn't know what I had gotten myself into.

The people were friendly, but I thought, "What in the world did I sign up for?". I was angry at God. I was angry at others in my life. I felt like everyone was against me, and I had just found myself alone in this room. "What is the purpose of getting through this?", I thought. I walked over to the window and looked out at the trees and pond. I became restless, walked over to the other side of the room, and looked in the mirror. Hating what I saw, restless I became once again.

A few minutes later, I was sitting on my bed, opening my Bible to the one chapter that always comforts me: Psalm 91. That afternoon, I found refuge in my God.

"Whoever dwells in the shelter of the Most High will rest in the shadow of the Almighty. I will say of the Lord, "He is my refuge and my fortress, my God, in whom I trust."...He will cover you with his feathers and under His wings you will find refuge; His faithfulness will be your shield and rampart."

If you are struggling today and if you need to find a safe place...cry out to God. Find refuge in Him. He is there. He does see you. He does know your hurt and your struggles. God is so faithful and He will protect you. I pray that you can find peace today. The peace that the Holy Spirit gave me that day. Whoever you are, wherever you may be, I am praying for you today as I write this. Keep fighting. Don't give up just yet. You can do this. God is on your side. Be still and let Him fight.

A month and a half passed, and I was sitting in my therapist's office. It was March 16th. Not that that date matters to anyone else, but for me, that reality smacked me in the face and punched me in the stomach. It was the day I was told I had an eating disorder. Why is that so significant? Someone finally saw what I was struggling with and called it what it was. They put a name to my pain. I sat in my therapist's rectangular-shaped office, curled up in a chair adjacent to her dark brown desk, staring at her bookshelf, trying to keep it together. I knew I probably had issues with eating. Even in treatment, people would comment on my plate at lunch and laugh at my portion sizes. It's one thing to know that you're struggling. It's a whole different thing for it to be seen, called out, and later told, "We have to call your parents." The thing was, the current treatment center I was at was for mood disorders. Their plan was to send me elsewhere to get help for the eating disorder.

That somewhere ended up being in Florida. Within a few days, I was sitting on the floor of the airport, waiting for the plane to arrive at my gate. I pulled out my white journal with a button on top and wrote. Writing in the middle of the storm...that's where I met God.

As I was sitting on my hotel bed alone that night, the room was silent. The TV wasn't on and I wasn't posting on social media or catching people up on the latest. Nobody knew where I was besides family. I was simply sitting there in silence when I felt the Holy Spirit so clearly whisper that it was time to start writing for people to read. I just sat there as thoughts flooded my mind. I'm about to enter my second (of nine... I just didn't know) treatment center...what is there to write about? That's exposing and vulnerable.

The next day, I took a taxi to the treatment center, and the rest is well, in this book.

But after I left that second treatment center in Florida, I began writing and specifically blogging. Sharing my thoughts in the middle of recovery. It was purely out of obedience to my God. I didn't want people to know the details of my story, but there was a grace to share it. I began to say that if it helped one person...just one...it was worth it to me. And I realized I began to find that one person who would read my blog or social media post. I found it worth it. There was purpose in my writing.

By the time I left Florida, I landed back in Georgia at yet another treatment center. I'd say this is where I had an encounter with grace. My therapist would always remind me to give myself grace. Almost every day I saw her, I heard those words. I was a mess. I beat myself up over nothing. I was never kind to myself. I didn't know how to show love to myself. I hated myself. Grace was the last thing that was on my mind to offer myself. But I liked my therapist and I knew that if she was telling me something consistently, it must mean something. I took it into consideration. Every day after treatment, I would find my way to a coffee shop closer to where I was living and order a honey lavender latte. It became my signature drink while I was in Atlanta. I became friends with one of the baristas there. I would sit and write about my day or write a blog post that I would publish later that afternoon. I attempted to embrace the place I was in and give myself some grace.

But she wasn't the last person to tell me those words. Practically all of my therapists have said so. "Give yourself grace". TR was the first to tell me. It seemed like every time I was in her office, she would remind me of this. I heard it from a therapist at Duke, and every therapist in between. Most recently a therapist said to me, "Give yourself grace, but don't give your eating disorder grace." Hearing this, all the while thinking to myself, "If I knew how to give myself grace, I probably wouldn't be in this place at all." I am obviously not giving myself grace as I think these thoughts. Why is it so hard? Why can't I just give myself the grace to "be"? Why do I feel the need to be in a place other than where I am currently in my journey? To that question, I can say this: looking around at others — and at a world that imposes a specific timeline for milestones like completing a degree by 22, getting married by 25, and buying a home by age 30, it's easy to find reasons to beat yourself up, be hard on yourself, and compare yourself to other people...which simply will get us nowhere. Give yourself grace to just be. Give yourself grace to be right where you need to be. Give yourself grace when you find yourself in a place you didn't think you'd ever find yourself in. Give yourself grace when you mess up, but don't let those mess-ups begin to lead you. Be gentle with yourself. Be kind. After years of beating myself up over the fact that I was "behind in life," or had found myself at yet "another treatment center," or had relapsed with an eating disorder, I am beginning to settle into the fact that who I am is enough, Annie, right now, in this moment. Enough. And I should make room for grace. There's always room for grace.

God of the Littlest Details

My sample perfume shattered on the floor before my eyes. Little glass pieces could be seen all over. Perfume covered my bathroom floor. The scent filled the air. It would have been an ordinarily clumsy moment if anyone else were to observe this. It was a sample. One of five. So tiny. But my mind began questioning. Which was it? Which dropped? Hopefully, it's not one of my two favorites. I looked at the four still intact and couldn't recall which was missing...making itself known with its sample scent all over the floor. I bent down and began cleaning up the broken pieces. One of the more significant pieces had black letters, and as I picked it up, I read "core mem." I had dropped the perfume "core memory."

To anyone else, it would've been trivial. But for me, the name was significant in this season and in that specific moment. It was strikingly significant. To me, what happened and what it had represented was just as significant.

Core memories have brought me to the place I am in today. Recovering from an eating disorder, battling daily with panic and a diagnosis of PTSD. Core memories. "A set of memories that hold emotional value," I have read elsewhere. The definition could take your mind to core memories that are good or not so good. I knew as soon as I saw the name this was about memories of moments that have wrecked my life.

This morning, I felt the Lord kindly reminding me that the memories I have held in my hand so tightly — having memorized their scent, looking at them as if the whole picture is right in front of me — will soon fall to the ground and be unrecognizable in the way they were always known by me. This morning, it was as if core memories were being shattered to pieces, unable to be pieced back together by me. It felt like a prophetic act in a way, not by me, but by God. He is intentional. This felt intentional. I was seeing Him in the details of that moment.

He was in the details of my perfume being shattered on the bathroom floor. He was found. I couldn't miss Him in the middle of the mess on my floor. He was seen as I was cleaning up the shattered pieces, and He reminded me that my core memories soon wouldn't be recognized by me. They might seem so vivid in my mind right now. The fragrance so strong will soon fade away though. Soon, the fragrance won't be so weighty in the room. The memories will soon become faint. It's not that they won't matter, but they will have shattered. All that has happened matters to my Father. And that's why He patiently and persistently whispers, "Trust me with this." It's not for me to figure out. The details are for Him. He is in the details. He's there.

...carefully into His hands. He will hold the broken pieces. He will be the only one to put pieces back together in a way that has the words, "and we know that for those who love God all things work together for good, for those who are called according to his purpose" woven through the story. All things. For good. That is a golden thread. That includes those core memories. I believe it to the very core of my being. The memories that have wrecked me will be used for good. Not one piece missing from His sight. All of it. Pieced back together into the most beautiful tapestry that only He could create. A story that could bring only Him glory. Only Him. He brings the healing.

In the same way that my hand clumsily gave over the perfume to the floor, I will yield and yield again to the Lord. But more intentionally than my hand gave the "core memory" perfume to the floor. I will give and give again at His feet. Giving these memories over to Him. Not holding tightly to them but giving Him full permission to do whatever He wants with them, with me, and with my mind.

It's safe to say I have only begun to heal from trauma and things that have been deeply rooted within. Trauma can be complex; this journey is wild and I am letting go of my need to understand how my healing will come. But one thing I know is that I can surrender and yield my "why" and "how" to the Lord. I can yield my "how" to Him as I think about Him as Jehovah Rapha — my Healer. I can go about my morning routine, breaking perfume on accident, pouring out oil intentionally on His feet, and be reminded that God's still in all of this. In every detail. In every core memory. In every moment. He is so, so very sovereign. What a God I get to love, serve, and make known. I am in awe.

This morning, picking up the broken "core mem" glass piece off the floor, I saw God in the details — all while wearing my t-shirt that says "sound mind". Once again, God is in the details — a God of the details.

Who knew 6:49 a.m. reminders through a little sample bottle of perfume could be so powerful? This morning, it was me.

Stay With Me

On June 30th, 2023, I was marked by a vision I had. In this vision, Jesus was leaning over me, saying, "Stay with me, Annie, stay with me." His voice was calm, yet His voice carried an urgency to it. It reminded me of something a paramedic would say to someone when they want them to stay alert and conscious. It was like Jesus was saying, "Stay with me" leaning over me, wanting me to keep my focus on Him. Wanting me to keep my eyes on Him. Wanting me to keep my gaze locked on His. Stay with me, Annie. Stay with me. Stay in my presence. It's your lifeline. It will bring you back to life. Just look at me. Look at me, Annie.

Journal entry — January 23rd, 2023: "I long to know the power and love of His gaze — not ashamed of me. He already has His eye on me. I want my life to reflect the reality of my gaze meeting His and never looking away."

Journal entry — May 25th, 2023: "Beauty on the narrow road. Somehow, there are fewer distractions, and there's more to see. Father God, I pray that you can strengthen my gaze. Narrow is the way that leads to life. On the narrow path, distractions fight for my attention, but they lose their power. They grow dim as I am walking hand in hand with my Jesus. There's more to see because I am not blinded by the things of this world. There's more to see because as my gaze is set on Him, I can see where He is looking. His guiding, loving, leading eyes. Leading me to places and to people I have never known existed. His eyes — full of compassion. His eyes — full of understanding. His eyes — meet mine, and I know I am known. Every detail of my life. It brings me peace, not fear. Questions fade as I gaze upon His face.

Journal Entry — June 20th, 2023: "I have come to know His love. I see it in His eyes, and I hear it in his voice. I hear His song over me, and I get caught up in the melody of Heaven. I dance unhindered by the weight and constraint of sin and shame. A hallelujah flows from my mouth. Holy holy holy becomes my anthem. I see the Lord, and I am captivated by His beauty. I can't seem to look away. Face to face. It's unlike just hearing stories of glory. My gaze meets His gaze. I could do this for all my days. His gaze. Eyes of fire. They pierce. They plant within me a hunger. They draw me in. Gazing into his eyes, I see what He sees. I see those in the world that He sees. I find safety in His gaze. I find protection in His gaze. I find love in His gaze. I am acquainted with a sound mind when I live in His gaze. I am never looking away. It's in looking to Him that I get to dance with Him. It was also in looking to Him and looking away from Him, that I found freedom, then chains again."

In early March, 2017, I wrote,

"A little over a month ago, I had a vision. I believe it was the Holy Spirit showing me the freedom that was available — the freedom I would experience not even two weeks later. I want to share this because I believe the Father wants everyone to know that this freedom is available.

As I was lying in bed, I saw a girl in an empty room. She was standing there wrapped up in a bunch of shiny red ribbon. It was wrapped around her so tightly that she wasn't able to get out. She was held captive and not able to move. Someone came and started unraveling her from this ribbon that was constricting her. She started dancing freely around the room. So confident. So free.

Two weeks later, I went to a church worship night. Someone was praying with me when they saw me dancing freely. I knew that what I had seen not even two weeks before was real. I knew this freedom was possible. My arms were up. I was ready to receive it. I knew that it was available, and it was mine.

I saw that shiny red ribbon and thought it was enticing. I was attracted to it. However, I now know that it symbolizes the enemy's lies, toxic thoughts, temptations, and other idols that I put before God.

For me, one of those things was the eating disorder. It was the thought that I would be worth something once I reached a certain weight or looked a certain way. The desire to be in control led me to be completely out of control in the end. What I thought I could use to gain control (the eating disorder) led me to spiral out of control and into captivity. Those thoughts, lies, temptations, and idols...believing them and agreeing with what the enemy and world were saying led me into captivity.

I thought I could get out on my own... but this vision was showing me that I couldn't do it on my own. I needed help. I needed someone's help to free me... in that vision, I believe it was Jesus who was unraveling me out of captivity and into freedom. He was unraveling me from the fear, depression, eating disorder, and lies, leading me into peace, joy, confidence, and freedom in Him. Finally, there was clarity about whose I was, and from that, I was able to see who I could be.

I was not just walking in freedom, but I was dancing in freedom.

I share this because I know God's desire is for everyone to be free. He wants everyone to dance in freedom, knowing whose they are.

He wants everyone to be free from the fear and lies of the enemy. Those thoughts and fears will still come, but we have authority over them. We have power over them, and they don't have to control us, leading us into captivity.

It's amazing how much freedom is actually possible when we finally realize whose we are — we become healed, redeemed, and freed."

So I wrote this out. I was living in freedom. I slowly stopped going to my appointments, got off all my medications, and moved to California. I felt like I could breathe again for the first time in years. I had been treading water in the storm for so long, unable to keep my head above the water, but I finally touched the ground. The storm had stopped, and the sky was clearing. When I was broken, and in bondage, I didn't know if freedom was what I wanted. It was like I had made a home in a prison cell, and in one of the cracks on the floor, there was one little flower growing. The light shone through to that spot. The prison cell didn't seem all that bad. It was all I knew. It was home to me. What I didn't realize was that just outside that window that I couldn't look out of, but not even 10 feet from where my prison cell of a home was, there was a field of wildflowers. One invitation of "coming away with the King" and I had tasted freedom. I knew that that was what I was created for. I wasn't created to live my life struggling with an eating disorder. I was created to be free.

But recovery isn't linear. The freedom was real, but it was very much just a remission from all the things I struggled with. As soon as I began to have memories of abuse, I felt like I was shot down, and I went back to my old ways. The thunder rolled, and I sought cover. I went back to the home and ways of coping I had always known. I became distracted by the noise of this world and lost my gaze.

Those three years weren't for nothing, though. I am thankful that in the midst of my depression, I found relief and joy again. I am thankful that in the midst of the eating disorder, I knew it was possible to become completely free. Not just coping but being completely free. Those years gave me hope. They gave my family hope. And I think they probably gave others hope who had been part of this journey as well.

At this point, I had moved back to North Carolina and was seeing a therapist weekly. Everything about my sessions with her was wrapped in peace outside of my average state of anxiety. Her office felt like a home, and she was the most non-judgmental person I knew. I was so thankful she was in my life during the time she was. But I struggled a lot. I lost focus and continued to seek out things that were only bringing death upon me. My OCD ran rampant, and exercise was out of control. I was suicidal, and I found no purpose in living. I had lost all focus on my Jesus, the one who brings life and purpose, which brought me to a place of desperation again.

Always an Invitation

A lways an Invitation
    There's always an invitation.
We are always invited.
To come away with,
to dine with,
to behold,
to gaze upon His beauty,
to never lose sight of Him.
There's always an invitation.
We are always invited.
Will we say yes?
Yes, to coming away with Him.
To dancing with Him.
To dining with Him and simply being with Him.
To beholding Him.
Losing sight of all but Him.
Hand in hand.
Never alone.
The invitation soon becomes an exaltation.
My hands are in His but my hands are held high.
Catching a glimpse of His beauty.

How could one not?

Holy, holy, holy.

One with the angels. Exalt His name on high.

My body is overcome just thinking of this.

The simple yes that is held in the invitation holds an eternity of communion when we grab hold of it.

As if our life depended on it. As if our life depended on it.

...an eternity of communion with the only one found worthy.

Will we say yes?

He is worthy of all that has to be left behind in order to say...yes.

And so I run.

I dine.

I behold.

I gaze.

I dance.

— upon injustice and disappointment.

I hear Him say, "Don't lose heart," and I catch His.

I catch His heart for the lost, weary, lonely, outcasts, and insecure.

Gazing. Gazing upon Him, I see what He sees. Being so near, I feel His heartbeat. I hear His heartbeat. I get caught up in the rhythm of His heartbeat, and I dance to its rhythm.

I rest to the rhythm of it.

"Peace, be still."

Being in alignment with Him is everything.

Beating in alignment with His heart is everything.

Saying yes to this invitation is saying yes to Life.

Wow, what an invitation we get to receive, and oh, if we dare, hand in hand with Him, we get to say yes.

A literal, life-altering, eternity changing, yes. We aren't alone in choosing this yes.

He is with us each breath and step of the way.

Remember, this yes holds eternal communion with the only One worthy of our yes.

There's always an invitation.

We are always invited.

Will we say yes?

He sits with me, and I hear His whisper, "Just look at me, Annie." I realize I was created for this. And this is the place where I will live from. My life declaring the reality of Psalm 27:4: "One thing have I asked of the Lord, that will I seek after: that I may dwell in the house of the Lord all the days of my life, to gaze upon the beauty of the Lord and to inquire in his temple."

Seeing Jesus has changed the way I see myself. Clean, pure, washed, holy, justified, righteous, full of life. Only by the blood can I live in this reality. I am so thankful that none of this can be undone.

Sacramento, California

It was at this point I was introduced to a residential program that houses women for six to nine months and walks them through freedom that's only found in Christ. Once accepted, I boarded the plane to Sacramento, California. I had no idea that I would be there for two weeks short of a year. I remember looking outside my window seat to a sunrise and hearing the Holy Spirit's whisper, "The One who raises that sun can carry your weight." He was reminding me that He could handle all the things to come. He could carry my weight. I could come to Him. And I would come to Him.

I had no idea what to expect entering into this home on September 8th, 2022. It was 111 degrees out and not the ideal welcoming weather. I had already seen God in the details of my conversation with the lady who drove me to the home, but I was about to step into a whole year of God unveiling Himself to me as a God who cares about the littlest things. A God so vast showing up in the details of my life. It fills me with wonder.

To say that I saw God in the details of that day would be a complete understatement, though. I think my jaw dropped, and I said "Dang" the moment I found out that my therapist had gone to the same ministry school as me. "Dang" because God is just cool like that. It meant a lot of things to me, but mainly that God had gone before me in this and put the right people on my path for this journey I was on. I found God in the details of that moment. The same day I met a girl who lives about thirty minutes from me back home on the other side of the US. We became sisters fast. I also had seen God in the details when my roommate told me that she deep cleaned my side of the room before I arrived.

In all honesty, I showed up at this home, exhausted, distracted, stuck, and scared. I had no vision for what I wanted and didn't know how to get out of the place I was in. I just felt like this was the next best thing to do and God met me where I was at. He met me in the mundane, He met me in the details, and He met me in all of my moments of "choosing." Whether I was choosing Him, choosing new thoughts, choosing to forgive, or choosing to use my authority — He was making Himself known in the most beautiful way. As much as God was making Himself known, I continued to wrestle with God, wanting to do things my way. It felt like there were more days where I knew panic rather than peace. There were many sleepless nights and wondering if any of it was going to be worth it. I had a hard time letting down walls and trusting the staff. I had to intentionally choose to let them in and allow them to partner with me in my healing journey. I am so thankful for the staff that walked alongside me that year.

For the majority of the first six months, I had the most incredible roommate. Once she graduated from the program, there were more room changes, and I eventually ended up having my own room.

I moved to a room across the hall that I liked to think of as the "rainbow" room. Every morning, if you looked closely enough, a rainbow would stream from the bedroom onto the floor in the hallway. It reminded me that my God is a promise keeper. Each morning, I would wake up to an alarm at 6:05 am and begin my morning routine. This included reading scripture from my "GCP" book.

God's Creative Power. I still to this day pick up that little booklet. Declarations based on scripture.

Sitting at the end of my bed, I would take the time to watch the world around me pass by. Without fail, every morning at the same time, there was a man who walked his dog. The dog, without hesitation, stopped in the same place every day before crossing the street to the park. In the springtime, my window would be open, and the most beautiful pink blooms would be rising on the bushes. We'd eat breakfast around 7:02 a.m. each morning. 7:00 a.m. really. But to have breakfast on the dot was never truly a reality. My roommate and I would occasionally be on kitchen duty and always made sure we had enough brown sugar oatmeal out for the two of us.

We did chores that we called "details" and got to clean the home each morning after breakfast. Cultivating the space so generously given to us, I saw it as an act of worship as well.

One day in the middle of July, I noticed the man wearing the hat and walking the dog again. I noticed they took their time. They weren't rushed. On this particular morning, he took a moment to observe the cement truck across the street at one of the homes. Something was different about that man. What struck me was he walked as if God had his back. I could notice it from inside the fenced-in yard. He knew God. I wanted to have a conversation with that man. Yes, strangers, that I was and that he was. But to live from a place of rest in God, so much so that people looking out their windows can notice? I wanted to learn from him!

That morning, the sun pierced softly through the branches into my room. It wasn't invasive in a rude way, yet it made itself known to all of me and the corners of the room. I could see the flowers outside my window — dark pink, light pink, purple — all kissed by the light of the sun. I was slowing down and in the slowing down, I was seeing God. I was seeing Him in the little details. It's safe to say that that man saw God in the details as well.

A few days later, I remember sitting outside in the backyard. Running my hands over the sparkles in the cement. The breeze blowing through the leaves of the trees, the wind gently flowing into my hair, and softly hitting my face. I felt it, yet it felt like nothing. Fierce and kind. Blowing through the grass I sat on. Birds happily dancing in the sky, singing their songs. The scent of coffee roasting next door — kindly and unapologetically making its appearance in the backyard. Introducing itself daily. Some days stronger than others. If you walk out after just taking a shower, no doubt your hair will smell just like it. The coffee will be generously donated to the home in the coming weeks. One memorable moment, lying in the grass with two friends, gazing at the stunning sunset. At that moment, I was catching a glimpse of heaven and the joy of the Lord. The skies proclaimed so brilliantly... I whisper, "Oh God, do it again."

It's Sunday evening, so we make our way upstairs. It's 7:28 p.m., and we are sitting waiting for scriptural declarations, as we do on Sunday nights. Writing seven scriptures for the week. Sitting there for a split second, I come to my senses, and nothing about it seems casual. These words are alive and active. They are sharper than any two-edged sword. We wait with anticipation. Finding out what truth we wait to cling to. Truth that will mold us, shape us, and strengthen us. I whisper, "Open up my eyes to see this greater reality you call us to live in. Truth. Let it live in my mind. Infuse my mind. Let the Truth that sets free, free me."

From Bitter to Sweet

My heart was bound. I had built brick walls to protect myself from those who hurt me, but in reality, I was only hurting myself. Unforgiveness. Anger. Bitterness. I had built walls around my heart to protect myself over the years, but I didn't know that within the walls were poisonous weeds deeply rooted and coming after my heart. I felt comfortable, and I justified it all. I was numb. I began to drink my own poison without even realizing it. Yet what was happening was slowly constricting my heart and killing relationships wherever I went.

I didn't know how much my heart was bound and wrapped in the chains of unforgiveness until I was free.

While at this home in Sacramento, we went through different "Keys to Freedom" during our counseling sessions. "Choosing to Forgive" was one of the keys we had to go through. Looking back, I would rephrase that and say, "We got to go through that key". It wasn't the burden I thought it was going to be. But at the time, I wasn't looking forward to it and felt like it was in the way of all the freedom I needed to find. In reality, this is where my freedom was going to be found. I just had to yield to the process.

I was assigned to read a book on forgiveness before starting this key. In my book response to my therapist, I wrote,

"But at this moment, the idea of forgiving — without them understanding or acknowledging the pain I am in, the time that was lost or my health that was lost is more painful than anything. And it feels impossible. I know that God is ready, waiting, and wanting to help give me the strength to do this. But He also allowed all of this to happen — in His presence? ...thinking of X is the last thing I want to do anymore...I'm scared to choose to forgive, knowing that when I do — especially X — I am releasing him — and control...I am just afraid to release others fully without them seeing and understanding what they have stolen."

After another book response, I wrote:

"I think I've known that there is unforgiveness that I still have — but I have justified it. And in ways, I felt that it's protected me when it's probably done more of the opposite...it still feels hard to simply forgive. To drop it and allow God to be my vindicator in His timing — following Jesus on the narrow path, I should forgive simply because doing so would be obedience to Him. But it doesn't feel simple right now. ...part of me wants to know what life could look like if I said yes to forgiveness in every area and relationship, but I feel stuck right on the edge of it. I didn't realize how much hatred or disgust I had towards myself until I started to think about all that had been done to me. I know there must be freedom on the other side of this — letting go of the pain, but whatever I am holding onto feels impossible to let go of. I feel like, in a way, by letting go and "dropping it," I'm letting go of my story, letting go of any chance of justice, my voice being heard, being understood, and letting go of healing. But I also feel like God is saying that it's only in letting go that He can move fully in all of it — and those things will be seen...I want to be quick to forgive. I don't want there to be a second thought in my mind. I want to be able to forgive when those who have inflicted pain know exactly what they did or have no idea what they did. I want to be so free within my heart that I can let go of the need for them to understand what they've done or the pain they've caused. I want to have the courage to forgive for no reason other than obedience — praying what Jesus prayed, "Father, forgive them for they know not what they do" — allowing that to be a bridge for me to come closer into a relationship with Him — giving Him space to show me His perspective — giving me eyes to see others the way that He sees them."

At one point amid my journey in Sacramento, I remember thinking, "If I came to this home just to know the power of forgiveness, it would've been worth it." We went through different keys to freedom during my counseling sessions. Leading up to this key, as you can tell from my journal responses, I had wanted those who hurt me to understand the pain that they had caused me. I lost years of friendships, school, and work, all due to the pain that was done to me and how I responded to it. I felt I needed these people to know what they had done.

But God. He knew that, and He went before me in this process of becoming free.

On January 31st, things changed in my heart forever.

In a counseling session one day, I read my Jesus' words: "Father forgive them for they know not what they do." As my therapist asked me what that meant, my initial thought was, "Mmm, good question." But I began to realize that Jesus didn't need the world to know what they were doing or the pain that they were causing Him in order for forgiveness to flow from His heart. He was interceding on their behalf, asking the Father to forgive them. For me, I had always wanted people to understand the pain they caused me. I never wanted to be misunderstood. It was a fear of being misunderstood, and I couldn't stand it. But reading that scripture changed it all for me that day. People didn't need to know the pain they caused me or the years lost because of what they did to me. I can choose to forgive them even when they don't understand the reality of what they did.

Jesus' reality on the cross gave me strength.

Woven throughout these few sessions, I had made a list of people I wanted to forgive.

The first week in March, I walked up the stairs and sat on the black bench outside the counseling office. A little anxious as usual and unsure of what would be taking place that day, God had already started preparing my heart hours earlier without me knowing it. In my journal, I had written down the words whispered to me: "Freedom is on the other side of forgiveness." I didn't know that within that session, I would be forgiving people that I never thought I'd be able to forgive.

Next thing I know, I am sitting on the floor of my therapist's office as I lead us in communion. It's only by the cross that any of this can be our reality. It's only by the blood of the Lamb that extravagant forgiveness is possible. After taking communion and thanking Jesus for the reality of forgiveness, I began writing names down. Well, first, I ripped up the original list I made. My therapist had a cross set up on one of the chairs. She had pieces of paper all with a symbol of a drop of blood on it. I would write down the name of someone I was choosing to forgive, simply saying, "I choose to forgive X" and "X is covered by the blood."

Forgiving multiple people, including myself, my therapist helped me put the paper that had X's name under the cross. Right before forgiving X, she said, "Remember and look to the cross," and it helped strengthen me. I heard a whisper, "Why wait?" and without hesitation, I forgave.

Before leaving that session that day, as we both stood up to leave the room, my therapist looked at me and said, "Become acquainted with freedom." I had no idea how much freedom I was actually stepping into. I had no idea what I had just released myself from, but in the coming weeks, it would make itself known.

What took place that day was completely supernatural, and only by His grace and strength was I able to do what I did. He was present in that room with me that day.

It took every bit of strength within me to choose to forgive, but wow, I am so thankful I did. I even had a faint vision of Jesus holding the man who abused me. Jesus held him. Jesus had him. I was letting go. No amount of "people understanding pain or years lost to fill in the blank" could bring freedom. It would only be Jesus. I was letting go.

I made the choice to forgive those who hurt and abused me. Choosing to forgive was simply out of obedience but in the coming weeks, the effects of forgiveness were catching up to me in the most beautiful way. What forgiveness was doing in my life was heavenly and could've only been supernatural. I would try to find anger that I had always known towards certain people and I couldn't find it. There was a photo that I had that I wanted to give to my therapist to shred at the beginning of my time in Sacramento. But that photo became a photo that rested on my nightstand, serving as a reminder to pray for them. I tried to comprehend what was happening but it was passing my understanding.

The simple act of obedience was a bridge that allowed the Holy Spirit to move and free my heart and mind in a way that only He could. I saw my therapist in the lobby one day. I jumped up from the couch and went over to her, and all I remember telling her was that forgiveness was doing something in my heart. It was different. It was heavenly. And I couldn't not tell people about it.

Today as I look through some journals and remember things the Lord has done, I am finding myself extra thankful for the reality of freedom that awaits us on the other side of that simple but wildly courageous act of obedience — choosing to forgive.

I wrote, "I didn't expect for any thoughts towards him to change...I feel like my heart has softened some towards X."

"After choosing to forgive X, I still had memories resurface. Because of this, the "choosing" and "choice" to forgive felt absolutely impossible to walk out. I knew I needed to continue to make that choice — protecting my heart. And so I did. And am. But it's the furthest thing from easy."

And today — my take on forgiveness. I pray that if I ever saw the man who abused me again, that forgiveness would flow from my heart. I pray that I am quick to forgive and that I am known for a life full of rich forgiveness. While in Sacramento, that "Key to Freedom" simply felt like words on a piece of paper. But that ended up being the most powerful step in my counseling process.

Jehovah Rapha turns bitter waters into something so sweet. He heals. And He healed my heart. We broke down the brick walls, we took care of the poisonous weeds and planted something beautiful. My heart is free now.

And to the one who is reading this right now and knows they have found themselves in a similar place, I won't say forgiveness is easy but I will say it's worth it. It might be the most difficult thing you end up doing but the kindest thing you do for yourself. Release yourself from the poison that isn't worth carrying around. Take on the freedom that was paid for on the cross. Your heart will thank you.

July 18th, 2023

Journal Entry: I feel like I am coming to a place that I have been faced with multiple times while I have been here (in Sacramento) but haven't fully accepted. To think or say that I am thankful that those years with the X happened or that I am thankful for those seasons of pain, depression, abuse, and anxiety feels absurd, inappropriate, and wrong. It makes me feel like I am approving it. But if it weren't for those things, I wouldn't be so sure that only Jesus saves, delivers, and heals. I wouldn't be so sure that only Jesus is the answer. That only He satisfies. I wouldn't be so sure that God is El Roi, Jehovah Rapha, Emmanuel.

I am thankful for the story I get to tell.

I thank God that He is in my story, and the story has Him woven through every moment. Even when I missed Him, He was still there. Faithful, He is.

I am thankful that what has happened has allowed me to use my voice. I am thankful that it has allowed me to help other people feel less alone in their own struggles and to remember that there is hope. There is a life outside of an eating disorder, trauma, and depression. I thank God for the story that I get to tell. All because He is in it.

Snails and Stars – A Night at the Treatment Center

Nights were the hardest during treatment, and this night was no exception. "Annie to the med room. Annie, Annieee to the med room." I was being called up to take my night meds, which I took every night to help me sleep. Anything to help me get sleep these days. But that night, I wasn't ready to go upstairs to get my meds. I wasn't ready to go to sleep with my mind in the state that it was in. Flashbacks were coming in a persistent and wildly unwelcoming manner, as all do, and I couldn't shake them. I didn't want to fall asleep like this.

Sitting there as the staff member handed me my meds, I grabbed the clear cup of meds but I hesitated. I knew I wasn't about to take them. I did my best to tell her what was going on but I don't think I barely spoke. Shaking my head, scared, and most likely spaced out, I told her I wasn't going to sleep. I held onto the cup of meds with my hands shaking and unable to think straight. My body caught on to where my mind was already at, and panic took over. This specific staff member understood what was happening. "Do you want to go outside for a little bit? Get some fresh air?," she said. I nodded yes.

Almost everyone else was fast asleep, but we walked downstairs, through the living room, and out to the backyard. "Do you want to walk over to the basketball court? It's open over there and we can see the stars." Both of us could easily agree that that is one of our favorite things. Stars. The sky. Space. At that moment, it was easily agreed upon and we both knew it might ground me.

Psalm 136:9 came to mind in the midst of these flashbacks. The vastness of who my God is would soon enough become more overwhelming than anything else.

The basketball court was the most open area in the backyard, and although there was a short way through the grass, we took the long way around. The long way unexpectedly became even longer when we realized all the snails of Sacramento came out to the sidewalk that evening.

Keep in mind, I was just up in the med room, body and mind wrapped in panic and a flashback. We walked along the sidewalk, passing by the windows to the room where we ate our meals every day, and walked around the corner so we could see the stars in an open area.

But let it not be forgotten, we saw the snails before the stars that night. Every. Snail. of. Sacramento.

The long way to the basketball court took us upon hundreds of snails that all came out to play that night. I honestly hated snails up until that moment (not that I loved them when I came across every one God created), but there was no going back and it was an "it is what it is" moment. We were in it deep. We had to intentionally tip-toe over the snails in order not to hurt them, and our laughing made it a million times harder not to step on them. "Oh no! Oh no!" any neighbor would be able to hear as we both laughed our way to the destination. The time it took, you would've thought we were walking miles. I stepped exactly where she stepped. Joy goes beyond circumstances, and I was able to laugh even in the midst of such darkness in my mind at that moment. The meds and the memories were at play that night, but so were the snails and the stars. I got to choose what to meditate and fix my gaze on, and doing so changed everything that night.

We finally made it to the basketball court. A sigh of relief, and shared laughs took place as I think we both hoped we didn't step on a snail or five. Looking up into the abyss of the sky, I was grounded. I was lost in wonder and full of awe. The heavens declare!

At first, I was completely aware that I was standing on the basketball court in the backyard of the treatment center, having just stepped over one hundred snails to get there. I was battling the anxiety of having to soon take medicine to go to sleep, and I was scared of the thoughts in my mind. But then I became lost in wonder. The memories and the idea of taking medicine were no longer able to pull me inward as I looked upward. I began gazing upon beauty. Heavenly beauty. Oh, the heavens declare! The stars burst with delight for what they were created to be. The snails off in the distance now slowly moving about the yard and maybe wondering what just happened with those two people who just passed through. God's creation. Grounding.

I remember I was so lost in the stunning beauty of the stars that it brought me back to memories of being in Uganda and seeing a shooting star for the first time. It brought my mind elsewhere, all the while grounding me at once. The scripture "You keep him in perfect peace whose mind is stayed on you because he trusts in you." stirred in my heart along with "to gaze upon the beauty of the Lord." The beauty of the Lord is all around. His beauty simply surrounds.

That night was hard. To describe it as such doesn't even seem right, but I began setting my mind on things above —quite literally...only after the snail extravaganza, which was most definitely all over the ground. Setting my mind on things above and getting lost in the wonder of God's creation, I felt settled enough to go back inside to finish where we had left off with the medication.

"But you, O Lord, are a shield about me, my glory, and the lifter of my head. I cried aloud to the Lord, and he answered me from his holy hill. Selah. I lay down and slept; I woke again, for the Lord sustained me. I will not be afraid of many thousands of people who have set themselves against me all around." (Psalm 3:3-6, ESV)

I slept soundly that night only after setting my gaze first on the snails, then the stars, and then ultimately on the Lord. Always always always setting my gaze upon the beauty of the Lord. This one thing. No matter the circumstances. Forever good. Forever faithful. Forever with me. Emmanuel.

No matter the circumstances, gaze. He will never change. Nobody can take this one thing away from the one who believes. We can always look to Him. Finding He was always looking at us first. Seeing Him, we see He is near. And we don't have to fear when He is near. Wow, what a beautiful reality. Just simply stunning. He is simply stunning.

My Beloved is the most beautiful among thousands and thousands.

I am thankful for the snails, stars, and that staff member that night in Sacramento. That night and that moment are a reminder to me to always keep my gaze transfixed on Him. Finding things within creation that ground me and allow me to see Him. Bringing me back to the beautiful reality of now. I pray that whoever reads this will also be reminded that no matter the circumstances, you can set your gaze on the sovereign One. We can always look to Him. He will never change. He will never leave. Emmanuel.

And to the next stargazer on that basketball court, you're most likely out with a staff member. I hope you took the "long way" to meet all the snails of Sacramento. I am praying for you, and that you encounter the God who loves personal details...He is a God of the details. I am praying you see Him and delight in Him in those details among the snails and the stars, too. Getting lost in the only One worthy of our attention. Jesus reigns above it all.

Renewing the Mind

Renewing the Mind was one of the most impactful keys for me. My mind felt like an enemy for so long. Memories and intrusive thoughts would come and I would let them have their way. Fear paralyzed me and led me to panic and ways of escape, which ultimately was leading to death. As I worked through this key, God's Word was coming to life for me and I felt like I was reading scripture for the first time. I began to realize that I could actually choose what thoughts I meditated on. I have started to believe that even when storms surround me, my mind can be sound. Memories might make themself known but I don't have to be shaken. My God has not given me a spirit of fear but of power, love, and a sound mind. I can think on things above and as I do this, the enemy has no space to wreak havoc within my mind. I began to believe that He really does keep me in perfect peace when my mind is stayed on Him. My mind has become so much stronger as I have become acquainted with Truth Himself.

Some of the strongest lies I believed were about the Father. Towards the beginning of my time in Sacramento I would feel fear and shame as I read the story of the prodigal son. I couldn't stand the idea of being embraced by the Father so I distanced myself. But as I have encountered the Truth of who my God is, I read that story now, and my heart longs to be embraced by my Father. Seen, safe, heard, and understood. My Father celebrates my homecoming. He puts a ring upon my finger, and a robe upon my back. He puts His arms around me. He calls me "Daughter," and I believe it. There isn't a desire to pull away or hide from shame but rather yield, lean in, and hear what He has to say over me. He is patient, kind, and slow to anger. I am coming to believe that I am safe in His arms, and He holds me while I heal.

My Voice

My voice was something that I felt like I lost back in middle school. Fear and shame silenced me. Whenever I would speak, I was met with criticism, correction, and denial. I never felt heard or understood when I would speak. I came to hate my voice. While in Sacramento, I discovered that it is okay to speak up and advocate for myself. I came to realize that I can speak through fear and I can speak even when I am afraid. Fear and shame can't silence my voice anymore. I had lived with regret that my voice wasn't heard fourteen years ago when I was most vulnerable and unsafe, but while in Sacramento I was given the space to use my voice. Both for seventh-grade Annie and who I am now. I have begun to allow God to unlock my voice that was buried and silenced for too long. And I am excited to see how He will use it in the years to come.

One day, I walked into my therapist's office where I sat at her desk, not in one of her comfy chairs off to the side. We had "business to attend to," it felt like. Running my hands across her maple-colored desk back and forth, I attempted to manage my anxiety. We made a simple phone call back home to North Carolina as I used my voice for seventh-grade Annie. It was a very short, simple call, yet it took everything within me. My voice shaking, but my voice spoke strong. It felt like all my strength left me, but I finally got my voice back. After hanging up the phone, my therapist came over and embraced me. I didn't realize how monumental making that phone call would be, but as I look back at that day — that hour — the decision to speak out brought freedom and unlocked my voice that was locked up for too many years. I am so thankful for the support that surrounded me that day. My therapist and the Holy Spirit both with me as I learned how to speak again. Using my voice since then hasn't been easy. I am still learning to speak through fear and speak when I am afraid. But I am doing it. I am using my voice that I thought was lost. God is restoring my voice.

Surrender in Sacramento

While in Sacramento, I experienced Jesus reaching out with His nail-scarred hands and inviting me to come away with Him. "Invited unto death," but realizing that is where my life has been found. He showed me how to sit with Him in my pain. He showed me how I don't have to be afraid of the pain that I feel — both physically or emotionally. The Prince of Peace is closer still. He is right there in the middle of it all with me. In the moments where I feel the weakest, I meet the greatest Strength living within me. I might be weak, but God is so strong within me.

He showed me that He is acquainted with grief and suffering Himself. Because of this — the fear of being misunderstood is overcome by my awareness of being fully understood by Him.

Sitting with Him at the table He's prepared, He breathes new life into me. His life. Being in Sacramento, I found that I do have the desire within me to live. It's a new feeling yet I feel like this is what was always meant to be. He takes me by the hand as I dance under the weight of glory, not shame. Dancing under the reign of my King Jesus. Dancing upon disappointment and injustice. Dancing as I hear His songs of deliverance. Unhindered by fear of man but living with a fear of the Lord that directs my steps.

The author of my story — the One who declares, "It is finished." is also the one who whispers, "This is just the beginning of so much more." And I believe Him. There's more to my story. My freedom isn't just for me. My healing isn't just for me. Finding my voice isn't just for me. It's for generations to come. I am finally getting my life back and learning to dream again. So much of the future is the unknown, but this time around, there is no fear attached to it, just an expectancy of all that is to come as I am fully surrendered to His ways. I know the Lord is going to show up as He always has, guiding, leading, faithful, and true. The hope I am coming to know is a living, unshakable hope. My anchor is strong and holds within the veil. And this changes everything.

Why

"Hold onto your why, Annie. Your why is Jesus. Don't let Him go...hold onto Jesus, not the pain. Hold onto Jesus." All throughout my time in treatment centers, I would hear people say, "Find your why." Find something that will keep you motivated. Find the reason why you're doing what you're doing. Why was I choosing recovery? I would always say I was doing it for my family. For my sister. And all of those reasons are still true.

But my main "why" is Jesus.

Over the years in treatment, the one thing that most places lacked was Jesus. I couldn't talk about Jesus and be understood. I remember wearing one of my favorite light blue sweatshirts that said "expect God" on the front and back and offending a couple of people. I was known as the "Jesus" girl. But whenever we were in groups or conversations, Jesus was missing. He wasn't at the center. Nothing made sense without Him. Only He satisfies. Only He saves. I knew that the only way I would get through the eating disorder, depression, anxiety, and trauma would be if I held onto Jesus. He is the only one that made sense. While living at the home in Sacramento, I got an email one day from a couple that I deeply respect. The wife said, "Hold onto your why, Annie. Your why is Jesus. Don't let Him go," It was just the steady, strong reminder that I needed in that moment at the treatment center I was living at during that time. My "why" could take me through any storm. My "why" could take me through any counseling session. My "why" could take me through any confrontation. It was Jesus. Jesus was the answer. I wanted everyone else in the treatment center to know just how close our Jesus was to us. That email was so simple to send on her end but it was such a powerful reminder that I clung to during my time there and continue to cling to.

It is Finished

June 6th, 2023, "Can I live in the reality of, "It is finished."? Can that be enough?"

Fight for the truth even when it doesn't make sense. Choose life. It is finished, it is done. It doesn't feel finished but that is a lie. It is finished. Jesus took beatings for me. He took the nails for me. He took death for me.

"Can I live in the reality of, "It is finished."? Can that be enough? It has to be enough.

"What does it look like to live in the reality of, "It is finished."? Choosing life.

Knowing that His blood is strong enough.

I remember one Friday in June, at the home in Sacramento, when I had taken it upon myself to punish myself in some type of way. OCD was wreaking havoc as well. There was a moment when I sat in my therapist's office, and I made a comment about how I didn't feel like I was finished. Like a task wasn't complete. I wanted to punish myself again. I couldn't get rid of the feeling.

My therapist asked me a question that resounded and filled my mind and body with the fear of God. "Can you live in the reality of, 'It is finished.'?" Can that be enough?

I remember thinking to myself it has to be enough. It has to be enough.

This was a turning point for me, a moment when I became desperate for a revelation of the cross. What did all of this actually mean? What does it look like to live in the reality of, "It is finished."? Jesus took beatings for me, Jesus took the nails for me, Jesus took death on the cross for me. It is finished. It is done. And now I hear him say, "Run! You're free!". Jesus isn't expecting for me to be hard on myself now. To beat myself up over simply being me, Annie.

Ask yourself, "Can I live in the reality of, 'it is finished.'?" The end of something is the beginning of something else. What is it that you don't think is finished? Can today be a day of surrender and seeing the beauty of God in the beginning of something else? The beginning of something you were created to live in?

Counting Planes and Reigniting Dreams in Treatment

Almost every day during treatment, I would sit on one particular couch in the living room and read whatever book I was assigned by my therapist. If it was a Brennan Manning book — who became one of my favorite authors — I would also make room for a dictionary beside me to look up every other word on the page. Occasionally, as the blinds were open, I would watch planes go by. In the evening, as the sun would set, I would catch glimpses of the beautiful, stunning, heart attempting to leap out of the window, sunsets falling through the houses and field so brilliantly and softly.

But watching the planes...I would watch them go by and begin to dream. I would dream because I knew that the days within treatment wouldn't be my forever. I knew that anxiety, trauma, and an eating disorder wouldn't define me forever. I knew that someday I would be back on a plane to Uganda and also to the Middle East. I would be reaching the unreached. I would be telling people about Jesus — our only hope, our only deliverer, our life, our joy, our peace.

I also believe it was there that I began to dream again. Right there on that couch. I believe that seeing those planes sparked something within me. Hope, maybe. There is a life outside of this. One day I'll be watching a sunset from the window seat of a plane flying across the world, telling people about my Savior again. Their Savior. My heart leaps simply writing this.

My therapist was the one who challenged me in this whole "dreaming" thing. She would have me go up to the prayer room, sit with God, and just...well...she didn't have any other plans for me. I even asked her, "What do I do when I get there?". But if you know her, you know she loves being led by the Spirit. And she loved us to be, too. I had no agenda. I honestly felt fear going up to the prayer room, though. What have I done with my life? Look at where I am at compared to everyone else. People are getting married and having kids and I am being drowned by the last decade of my life. But I knew God had gone before me. I knew He was excited to dream with me — with me. Not for me. Plans, purposes, and a future. He would be in it. But He wanted me to step into it. Hand in hand. All of it would be with Him. And all of it would be for Him.

Dream again. It's unto something.

Even writing that is a wild thing to write. At eighteen, I didn't believe I would live to see nineteen. Each year, I lived as if I wouldn't see the next. Depression dragged me in and under. But I am living under the words of Jeremiah 29:11, which is a promise from God and living with the reminder that I have a choice in choosing life! Choosing to dream! I am so thankful for that window, those planes, vision, hope, my therapist who challenged me in that dreaming and also gave me those books that had me sitting on that couch reading and every once in a while glancing outside to gaze at the planes. So thankful. I have a necklace my sister gifted me this past year. It has "Jeremiah 29:11" written on one side and "hope + future" on the other side. She knows that my battle with the present and the future is real. She knows there is pain surrounding "life" and even the thought of "choosing life." But she knows the hope and future God has defined, destined, and written out for me is one worthy of being sought out and walked out. And so, one step at a time, hand in hand with the Lord, I am doing just that. This necklace is worn every day as a reminder to me of that truth. And it becomes a reminder and conversation starter to anyone else who compliments me on it.

He was restoring dreams and hope to my heart every time I would see a plane and think about being on one again someday.

Watching planes from that window was a little glimmer and a wild spark of hope. "It won't be like this forever." Soon, you'll be on a plane again. Soon — wrapped in God's timing — soon. He is in the waiting. He is in the dreaming. Intentionally being entwined as one with the Lord. I used to ask, "What is this unto?". Hope and future. My eyes are on Him.

I encourage you to find your "window" and look out. Remind yourself of the thing that has been forgotten about. The buried dreams. The thing you think you can't do anymore because of X, Y, Z. Ask God to make a way. He is a Waymaker, that I know. The things keeping you on the ground won't always keep you on the ground. The impossible is possible with our God. He's in the waiting. He's in the dreaming.

Held to the Flame

It was January 12th, 2023, and I was sitting in the back of the room in a treatment center. The back of the room is where I always sat. I could see everything that was taking place while also plan an escape route if I wanted to leave before others. It felt safe. That night, I was present but not fully present. A song was playing in the background, and about halfway through, I heard the words cut through the air so clearly and directly, making a landing straight on my heart. My Moleskine journal was open, pen already in hand, and I wrote down the lyrics.

"What will I say when I am held to the flame like I am right now?" Mercy Me

Pen to paper — "You are Emmanuel. You are omniscient. Within this pain ...Jehovah Rapha...yet to be uncovered. Yet to be discovered. Yet to unravel. Even still. Jehovah Rapha."

"Holding carefully the words... but still holding "You are good.""

"You are El Roi."

God with me. The one who knows all. The Healer. Even if I don't yet know it in my body doesn't change the reality of who my God is.

God is good. Even in the midst of things I have seen and the pain that I feel. Oh God, you are still good.

And El Roi, the God with me, also sees me. He sees me and He sees all that takes place. He has seen all that has taken place. All that has raised weighty questions over the years, but a good God who sees all also sees me and I take comfort in that — even in the blazing fire.

I might be held to the flame but I have never been so convinced that He is who He says He is.

What will you say when you're held to the flame?

Letter to Escape

E scape and all the ways you have presented yourself, just looking at my past and some of my present could speak to how you've shown up, existed, and impacted me. You've made yourself known to me and had your say but for far too long. It's time for me to now make myself known to you. Escape — you introduced yourself to me with a number of different names and faces — all of them having promises attached. You've shown up in my thoughts, mindsets, behaviors, and distractions. You've been present and with me when I felt nobody else was with me. You came in, offering a way out for me when I've felt trapped and stuck. You offered me an "answer" right before my eighteenth birthday when I layed in bed consumed with a fear of the future. You showed up as the thought that I could just take my life and avoid the future altogether. You came through for me when I felt overwhelming anxiety showing up at that volleyball tournament and I needed a way out. With you in mind, I acted out, refusing to walk into that convention center, and my coaches heard I was "sick." You provided an easy way out of anxiety at the moment yet somehow always created more for me. You showed up for me when I was so gripped by anxiety junior year of high school — you convinced me that if I just left the school — all anxiety would leave. You showed up for me with such comforting thoughts of suicide if I couldn't escape the anxiety at school. You did come through, temporarily, with relief from what I was feeling when I left mid-year and had the chance to go to public school. You came through, temporarily, when that week in public school became too much and I was pulled out and homeschooled. You came through once again at the start of Senior year when I couldn't handle the anxiety the night before the first day — you convinced me that it would be better to die than face that first day of school. My parents, once again, agreed to homeschool me. My family and pastors saw my words as manipulation when I hung onto this escape, but I really did think you'd help me. When anxiety and depression overtook me at the end of that process to go to college you promised an out. At community college the next year, with the end of the semester in sight, your promise was immediate, so I withdrew, only a couple of weeks left in the semester.

Your thoughts became more than relief in my mind. You came to life for me in all those moments with school and you even showed up that summer before ministry school when I couldn't handle anxiety. Suicide made sense. Escape. You failed me all the nights I tried taking my life and woke up. Either that or God saved me. I'd like to believe the latter. I clung to you and you backfired — with so many other ideas of providing relief and a way out. Self-harm — the relief I felt those nights in the bathroom when blades touched my skin. Medication — the nights I knew that if I took too much, I would feel okay. Showing up in the ways I used and misused medicines. You helped, but only temporarily. You made it so I always needed to reach for you again. Taking certain meds and sleeping the day away instead of eating. You were there for me when I started that one medication — making me feel dead to my senses yet alive all at once. Taking too much became a thrill, and watching the numbers go down on the scale each morning was satisfying. You made me feel good about something when people made me feel bad about everything else.

Escape, you've masked yourself as peace but I am realizing that you're chaos. You came through in all the ways that I felt I had to check things and do things in order to feel okay. I listened to you. Remember the volleyball tournaments? "Bounce the ball eleven times before you serve otherwise, the ball won't go over the net." "Use eighteen pumps of shampoo and eighteen pumps of conditioner every time I take a shower because I am eighteen." Soon, it turned to nineteen. I checked the outlets. I unplugged everything in my room before I left the house to go anywhere. I'd walk up the stairs a certain way or re-walk up the stairs a certain way so that so and so wouldn't "get hurt and die." Every time I left my car, I would usually have to go back to make sure I put the car in park. There was an eight month period of not being able to drive my car due to OCD thoughts taking over. Sitting in other people's cars, I would put down a layer, blanket, or jacket first because of contamination worries. All of this as an escape from anxiety. Doing these acts eased my mind, only for a moment. For everything, you made me feel in control. But just for a moment. In reality, you threw me out of control. You told me that I would feel peace if I read through all of the Psalms before I left South Africa — but in the midst of that goal to reach peace, my heart and mind felt like they were wrapped in anxiety. Escape, another face of yours, was exercise. Even in the midst of chronic pain, I used you as a punishment to my body.

I've kept you around in my mind simply because of your promises to me. In all that you have given me and helped me through over the years, you have also taken from me. You've taken so much but not too much that my God can't restore and redeem. I'm coming to find that the ways you've helped me run from pain, from reality, from memories, from fear, from shame — have kept me from running to the only One who actually has answers, freedom, and healing for me. The more desperate I've become to get unstuck even here in Sacramento, the more I am realizing you can't be present in any more of my steps forward. It's time to take you off the table. No longer leaving you as an option. It's time to say "no more" to you and let my whole life say "yes" to Jesus in a way I've never said yes to Him. And my goodness. If I have caught glimpses of His beauty as He has relentlessly pursued me — I can only imagine what is to come fully facing Him. You have provided a false sense of hiding but I am now saying yes to my true hiding place and refuge. You have provided a fake comfort and now I am making space to know the one who is Comforter. You have provided a cheap, shallow, and temporary satisfaction but now I am saying yes to the one who truly satisfies - satisfaction so rich, so fulfilling, so pure. "but whoever drinks of the water that I will give him will never be thirsty again. The water that I will give him will become in him a spring of water welling up to eternal life." (John 4:14, ESV) You have provided a fake empty peace but now I am making room for the Prince of Peace to come in. You've been a priority in my life for so long but my heart keeps hearing, "You shall have no other gods before me." The only one I have known to be trustworthy is speaking to me and I want to listen, not half-heartedly. It's time to clear the clutter you've come to be in my life and it's time to put my God back in His rightful place. I don't want to hear His voice, but look to you. You're not worthy of my attention or my, "Yes.". My "Yes." has value and weight, and I am giving it only to Jesus at this point. I desire to seek God and to live in His presence but I can't seek Him, seek His face, and do so with all my heart, soul, mind, and strength if I'm still clinging to your ways of fake, false, empty, temporary comfort. I've bowed to you for long enough but it's time that you are taken captive, brought into my God's presence, and obey Him. Unfortunately, you can't stand in His presence; you will bow and He will finally reign in all areas of my life. You've stolen, you've killed, you've destroyed. But Jesus says He has come to bring life — and life in abundance. Today, I am choosing Him. Today, I am choosing life. I'm no longer okay with saying, "Yes." to Him, stepping forward with one foot and allowing my other foot to drag with a ball and chain — hindering me from running the race set before me. I'm going to watch as He prepares a table before me — in the presence of my enemies — which I am recognizing includes you. I am saying, "Yes." to dreaming again without you having a say. I'm saying, "Yes." to my vision being restored — no longer blurred or tainted by your ideas and opinions. I'm saying, "Yes." to radical and rich encounters with love. I'm saying, "Yes." to knowing a peace that surpasses all of my understanding. I am saying, "Yes." to surrender. I am saying, "Yes." to my steps being strengthened and the promise "from strength to strength". Letting go of you, Escape, my arms will be free to worship the King of Kings and Lord of Lords — without hindrance, hesitation, or the fear that you have created.

In all the ways you have shown up in my life, you have come in shattering hopes and dreams, causing delay and causing more pain than you helped me push away, run from, and suppress. The other day, I wrote in my journal, "Wow, I don't want anything to keep me from Jesus anymore. I want my heart to be fully His. I can't stand the thought of being half in, half out anymore. I can't stand the thought of saying, "Yes." to following Him and Him seeing me turn the other way — not looking at Him — choosing to step towards death instead." As I thought about you and all you have done, my heart was longing for more of Him. You're already losing power. There's some really good news but maybe not for you. My God works all things together for good. Every detail. Nothing is hidden or missing from His sight. All is woven into a beautiful tapestry. So beautiful. The shattered pieces will be used for my good and all for His glory. The community and fellowship you made me lose in high school and even ministry school will be restored because that's just who my God is. The health you made me lose is only going to introduce me to God as Healer in a way I wouldn't have known if it weren't for the pain and heartache. The hands that were once a slave held captive to self-harm will soon create and write — carrying healing and freedom — and releasing it to those around me. Blades and clenched fists are being replaced with a pen. All will hear of Jesus that set me free from you. The feet I used to compulsively exercise with are yielding to the Holy Spirit. To step into rooms and countries to tell of a life that's only found in Him. You can find me walking in step with the Spirit, going places that you could never take me. My heart that took beatings is still beating. My brain that you tried to screw up, beat, and take out, is now in the position to receive and hear strategies from Heaven. I'm now making space for my heartbeat to come into sync with His. I am saying yes to gazing upon the beauty of my King. Inquiring in His temple all the days of my life. Ascending the hill of the Lord, with clean hands and a pure heart. I am saying, "Yes." to His daily bread, saying, "Yes." to feasting on His faithfulness. "Yes.", to the stunning reality of constant communion with my Jesus. "Yes.", to revelation and wisdom as the clutter, noise, and confusion leave. "Yes.", to hearing secrets and mysteries: great, hidden, mighty things. "Yes.", to the abundant life — to friendship with God. "Yes.", to being trusted by God. "Yes.", to living in the light, to living a life of integrity. Escape, I have clung to you as a lifeline but from this day forward, I am clinging to my Jesus. Although I feel like I am losing a ton with you no longer being an option for me, I just want Jesus. I need Him. So much more than I need you. I am going to give Him all of me. Allowing my fear to be consumed by His love, I don't have time to think about you anymore. I am ready for him to have all of me. He has all of me now.

Choosing life. Choosing Jesus.

- Annie

Breath In My Lungs

I became aware of the breath in my lungs this morning...and these were the thoughts that followed.

Breath. What a beautiful thing.
Coming into an awareness of my own —
My breathing. So steady. So strong.
It's a blessing, Not a curse.
It leads me to the thought, "I am alive."
I shouldn't be. But I am.
Within this breath is strength.
Within this breath is hope.
Within this breath is Him. Yes, Him.
Because He breathes life into me. His life.
The breath of life. The breath of God found in me.
God's breath, in me.
This breath.
So steady. So strong. So full of hope and a future.
Purpose. Yes, purpose.
Purpose in each breath even when it's not felt.
So full of life. My heart is beating.
To the rhythm of heaven. To the rhythm of life.
Abundant life. The life He created and destined.

Death defeated.

All because of King Jesus. And now life. Breath.

What a beautiful thing.

I don't know what led me to this awareness of my breath this morning, but what a beautiful thing. A simple, wildly significant, beautiful thing.

When It Simply Hurts to Live

O ver seven years ago, I was given the diagnosis of fibromyalgia. Some days are easier than others, but not a day has gone by that I haven't felt pain or fatigue.

When I was in a dark place, I remember thinking, "For each breath I allow myself to take, I am allowing chronic pain to continue in my body." I believed that giving up completely would be an escape from the chains of the pain. This pain. Spontaneous, sporadic, constant, stabbing, shooting, and sharp but so dang dull. I've lived with it for so long that when I feel the pain, I have almost grown numb to it. I feel it but it feels like it's just a part of me.

The pain drags me back and pulls me under. It's suffocating and, at the same time, reminds me that I'm alive. I can hardly imagine what a life of no pain in my body would look and feel like. Is that even possible? How do I get there? What would that look like? What would that feel like? Sometimes, I feel like the woman in Luke 8, knowing there is healing in His wings. Only His. But I don't even have it in me to reach out and touch the hem of His garment. My arms are too fatigued.

So, where do I find motivation? Where do I find hope? Where do I find the strength to keep taking one breath after another, even if it feels like pain pursues me? Well, some days it takes everything in me to get on my feet but sometimes and somehow I do it. It takes everything in me to take a shower, do a load of laundry, or cook a meal, but sometimes, and somehow, I do it. Although I am still trying to figure out what motivates me, I do know my hope is a living, unshakable hope. It's an anchor that holds within the veil that changes everything. I can feel the pain and have hope. I can feel the pain and not be moved in the storm. I can feel the pain and be thankful for the breath inside my lungs.

When it simply hurts to live, I hold my Jesus' nail-scarred hands and know that He is acquainted with grief and suffering Himself. He whispers to me that I am not alone and He is with me always. His presence changes everything for me. I am so thankful for my Jesus.

Holding onto Hope

I recently heard the words that hope can't be a part of a treatment plan. On a mission for all things practical, I can understand why that was said. I wrote down those words because it caught me so off guard...and in the back of my mind, I also knew I could write about it someday. Well, today is that day.

Hope. Treatment. I've had a colorful little journal that was pulled out during all of my doctor appointments over the last seven years. A promise journal, you could call it. It holds promises I have written down from God. People might call me crazy. People might think that's crazy. But it provided hope for me. It provides strength. And it's gotten me through some of the toughest doctor appointments. Hope isn't "fluffy and light." It's not "weak." The hope we have is an anchor. It's strong. Having hope is having strength. It allows us to be unwavering. Without hope, what is the point? Hope has to be a part of the picture when I think and talk about moving forward. It simply has to be.

I am thankful for the hope I have.

So, I'd like to say, "Hope has to be a part of the treatment plan."

Hope deferred makes the heart sick.

I'd like to say that hope cannot be forgotten when thinking practically in someone's treatment plan. If someone has been battling with a disease for years and years and all the people surrounding the person are simply burnt out, they just want to hear the answer. Find the answer, but don't let go of the hope you know. Hope that might feel hard to hold. Isn't that faith? You can't always see what you're believing and contending for. But isn't that faith?

The entire time I have had chronic pain and have sat in doctors' offices, I have also heard the Lord say, "Hold onto hope, for your healing is on the horizon." Do the practical, but don't let go of hope. Not for yourself. Not for the family member you're contending for. Don't let go of hope. Let hope fall into any and every area of the treatment plan. Let it be there. We make space. Hope is alive. Hope will not leave the room. At least not the room I am in. It will not leave the conversation. It will not leave my story. Hope is vibrantly alive and will always be welcome. Hope is an anchor. Hope is my anchor. Hope will always be a part of the conversation. And I am holding onto hope, for my healing is on the horizon.

The Day My Scale Didn't Recognize Me

I went inpatient, then to residential, then to php (partial hospitalization). Before entering inpatient, I was at my lowest weight and now I was recovering.

One day, in a session with my dietician, I told her I really wanted to weigh myself and thought that if others (providers and nurses) knew my weight, then I should know, too. We discussed it would be a slippery slope, and although down the road, knowing my weight wouldn't necessarily be a bad thing, right now, I simply wasn't in the place to know it.

The morning came when I was supposed to bring my scale to my dietician and it turned out that instead of going to php that day, I had another appointment. I still had my scale so I decided, "I might as well weigh myself while I still have it."

I stepped on my scale but my scale didn't recognize me.

The thing is, my scale records my weight in an app on my phone. It had all my previous history stored on my phone from before residential and inpatient on there. The moment I stepped on the scale, I was almost two and a half months into recovery and eating regularly.

The scale didn't recognize me and asked if it was the same person who was using it as before. I had to say, "Yes." before continuing.

Yes, it's still me! But healthier. And coming face to face with reality not allowing any denial to slip in, this "present" me had also gained a lot of weight.

All sorts of emotions shot up to the surface within a second and I was left in the moment. Just me and my scale.

What got me through the moments and days and meals after that?

It's been hard and it's absolutely been more challenging than if I were to have not weighed myself. Or I'll say, other challenges would have arisen instead if I made another choice that Monday morning. But the challenging meals and days have opened the door for me to find my why again. Why am I doing what I am doing? Why am I recovering? What motivates me to choose life and choose recovery day after day?

At this very moment, I am thankful though.

Thankful for how far I have come.

Thankful for how much growth I have had.

Thankful for a body full of strength and life.

Thankful for a body that is the temple for the Holy Spirit!

No matter the number on the scale and whether it's a mystery to me right now or not, none of that negates my worth, value or determines my future, which is full of purpose and hope.

And I hope that if you're reading this and you're in a similar place, you come to know the same. No number determines your worth. Never has and surely never will.

An Open Letter to My Eating Disorder

Where do I even begin? Where did we even begin? I don't remember a day when I sat down and said, "This is what I am going to live with for the next ten years of my life." But you made yourself welcome as if the door to my home was open to all. My relationship with food had always been normal until I caught a glimpse of you. Meeting you changed everything for me. My therapists over the years have asked if I wanted to name the eating disorder, and I never really got around to doing it because it just feels worthless. I'd rather you be nameless. You aren't worthy of having a name.

Written above you was the word "escape" for me, and that's what you were. An escape. I grabbed control when I grabbed hold of you, but in doing so, I would slowly spin out of control. Finding my worth in a number on the scale meant everything to me and would dictate what my day looked like. The first thought on my mind, when I would wake up, would be, "I need to weigh myself." If the number wasn't what I liked or it wasn't a lower number than the day before, I would beat myself up. Shame, embarrassment, and self-hatred were empowered by every step I took with you.

One day the OCD was shouting loudly and set a rule. "You can't eat before 5:00 pm."

For the next two months, my day consisted of everything but food until five o'clock, a salad at five o'clock, and then I was done for the day.

At the same time, I was also taking a prescribed medication at a high dose, which has known side effects of decreased appetite, which wasn't helping my situation. The next thing I knew, I was being admitted to another treatment center. It seemed like a never-ending cycle.

So, to you, anorexia, and all of your friends, I'd like to say, "When helping hurts."

You were a constant in my life over the last decade. One that I could always count on being there for me when the roads became rocky and the storms rolled in. I knew I could trust you with the outcomes you could provide for me. But plain and simple, you were only leading me to death.

I do remember at one point in my journey, I told one of my dieticians that I didn't care if this eating disorder killed me. I was so exhausted and beaten down. I simply just didn't care. But there's a hope, a purpose, a life that I see now that I couldn't see in that haze. There's a field of wildflowers just ten feet away and an invitation from my King asking me to come away with Him. To dance with Him. Freedom is possible. I'm sure you remember, but I had a three-year remission where you were out of sight and no longer in my life. My Jesus had all of me. All of my attention and affection. Treatment centers say that I'll always struggle with you to some degree or another, but those three years showed me that it's possible to be completely free. The answer: eyes fixed on the beauty of Jesus. Only He satisfies.

So, as I write an open letter I also might say this is a goodbye letter to you. I couldn't say bye enough times and be content. You ruined years of my life. You ruined relationships. You isolated me night after night and day after day. You destroyed my body. But as one of my former therapists would tell me, "Give yourself grace; don't give your eating disorder grace." There is so much grace to go around, but none for you.

And to anyone reading this open letter and finding themselves in a similar place, freedom is possible. Lean on those closest to you, look to the only One who can save you, and give yourself a little grace in this journey.

Reminders from the
"Master Treatment Plan"

A few years ago, I was going through a box of papers in my room. I don't think I had ever actually read those papers until that afternoon. As I was going through them, I found one that stuck out to me as if it was the only piece of paper actually there. It was from the residential treatment center I was at in Florida.

It said "Master Treatment Plan" dead center at the top in the biggest, boldest letters the document could have. It was from April of 2016.

The first things my therapist had written on that paper were my strengths and weaknesses.

The first things...my strengths and weaknesses. We can just say weaknesses because that's all I saw.

I will not deny it... they were absolutely weaknesses of mine in the midst of that eating disorder but it was no fun to see it written out. I want to share these with you. Those weaknesses aren't who I am. The words she used to describe me were not me, Annie Elizabeth Snyder. That eating disorder was not me, but the following words described how I responded to things in the midst of those struggles.

"distrustful"

"indecisive"

"not open/articulate"

It makes me sad. These were weaknesses of mine as I found myself engulfed by the eating disorder. In the midst of that eating disorder, I was not good at communicating and I was anything but open and able to trust her. I couldn't trust anyone. I lived constantly on edge. During that time, I was so full of shame that many of my therapy sessions were spent in silence as I intentionally made no eye contact with my therapist. I would sit there ashamed, feeling inadequate, and wanting to hide. The eating disorder led to shame, guilt, fear, and confusion. which led to another weakness listed... being indecisive. I know exactly what she was referring to as she wrote that word down. I wasn't able to make up my mind. Did I want to stay in that eating disorder, or did I want out? Did I really want to recover? The lies from the enemy were so blinding that I had no idea if freedom was what I wanted... or if it was possible.

Those were weaknesses of mine going through treatment and it was a vicious cycle.

The eating disorder led to anxiety, which led to panic attacks, which led to shame, which led to silence and hiding, which led to more shame, which led to more anxiety, therefore pushing me further into that eating disorder. You get the point. That cycle is vicious and toxic and went on for too many years.

Why am I sharing this with you?

Because God.

God can redeem, restore, heal, and free anyone held captive and hurting. Whether it's a sickness (mental or physical), any sort of oppression, shame, anger, jealousy, etc... whether you have struggled with it for ten days or ten years...our God can take that away.

Through experiencing freedom, I have started to learn who I am to my Father. Maybe in the world's eyes, those weaknesses were important to put in my medical records and treatment plans...I don't really know...but I do know one thing...those weaknesses, diagnoses, medication prescriptions, and hospitalizations were not me. That's not what the Father sees when He looks at His daughter. He longed for me to see myself the way that He saw me... not as the world saw me.

As I sat there on my bedroom floor reading this "Master Treatment Plan," I was reminded of something.

These will always be things that people see when they see my medical records. It's reality...and that can kind of hurt.

But it will only hurt and affect me if I look at it through the eyes of this world.

When I look at any situation or circumstance the way that the Father sees it, things will be radically different.

I look at these papers and no longer feel shame or anxiety. I don't feel hopeless or incapable. I am filled with hope, peace, joy, and love from the Father. I am smiling knowing that freedom is possible. Freedom from sickness and shame is so possible and available. God sees me and He sees His daughter as whole. He can restore. He can heal. Redemption is a beautiful thing.

Long story short, I was reminded of this Truth when looking at that "Master Treatment Plan."

My identity is in who God says I am...not those papers or that treatment center that I was admitted to.

Today, I am thankful that the "Master Treatment Plan" is helping me see my true identity in Christ. Let this be a reminder if you ever find yourself in a position where doctors begin putting labels on you. Acknowledge them, but don't take the labels on as who you are. You are not your anxiety, depression, eating disorder, or trauma. You were made for more!

Jehovah Rapha

One morning in April of 2017, right before I woke up, the Holy Spirit flashed an image of a banner before my eyes. On the banner, it said, "Jehovah Rapha."

It happened fast and was over within a second. At the time, I didn't know what the name meant but as I looked it up that morning, I was led to a story in Exodus. The Israelites experienced God turning bitter water into something sweet that they were able to drink. This miracle had introduced them to God as Jehovah Rapha.

Exodus 15:22-27, ESV —

"Then Moses made Israel set out from the Red Sea, and they went into the wilderness of Shur. They went three days in the wilderness and found no water. When they came to Marah, they could not drink the water of Marah because it was bitter; therefore, it was named Marah. And the people grumbled against Moses, saying, "What shall we drink?". And he cried to the Lord, and the Lord showed him a log, and he threw it into the water, and the water became sweet. There the Lord made for them a statute and a rule, and there he tested them, saying, "If you will diligently listen to the voice of the Lord your God, and do that which is right in his eyes, and give ear to his commandments and keep all his statutes, I will put none of the diseases on you that I put on the Egyptians, for I am the Lord, your healer." Then they came to Elim, where there were twelve springs of water and seventy palm trees, and they encamped there by the water."

I was in awe of what had flashed before my eyes that morning, knowing that it could only be the Holy Spirit that would've given that image to me. Every time I look back and remember this, I realize how strategic and intentional this was for Him to speak this. God went before me.

I started noticing pain in my body one day a couple of months later. It was 2017 and I thought to myself, "This isn't normal." I had no idea that the start of it wouldn't have an end anytime soon.

The morning He introduced Himself to me as Jehovah Rapha, the Lord spoke to me about who He was and who He was promising Himself to be for me.

Through some of the darkest, most painful nights, I have clung to this beautiful reality and promise of God being Jehovah Rapha. The reality of this brings me to a place of trusting His character and who He is because He says so. Not because I see it but because He says so.

I choose to trust in the mystery of it all, and my heart is overwhelmed with thankfulness, hope, and victory as I rest in the reality that my God has the final say in all of this. In this current season that I find myself in, He speaks over it, saying, "Jehovah Rapha — I am the God who heals."

I moved to northern California a year later and during that time, I was going through ministry school. What most people didn't know about me was that I was dealing with chronic pain and desperate for any kind of answer. I made an appointment with a doctor in Redding whose office was a few blocks from my apartment. The day of my appointment, I remember walking up there...scared. I wasn't in my hometown and I was about to see a new doctor, having no idea who he was.

This doctor listened to me describe all the symptoms of fibromyalgia that I had, and then he turned to me and said, "Can I pray for you?". My heart so unexpectedly leapt, and I let him pray for me in the middle of the doctor's office. It was the following appointment when the doctor handed me a piece of paper on my way out of the office in downtown Redding one morning and said, "We can check back in a year from now." Looking down at the paper, he had written a prescription for a pain medication that he said was not promised to work and added the words, "Due to losing options." The little bit of strength I had to go back to him once more looking for any more answers was ripped out from within me as he handed me that visit summary. He had gone to school for this and he was handing me a white piece of paper with no options, saying, "I'll see you in a year!"

I walked out that day, barely able to hold the piece of paper, and with tears streaming down my face, I called my mom, who directed me straight back to Truth within the first words that she spoke. At that moment, I did not care who saw me or what they thought. I remember one man on my right curious as to what was going on but I simply zoned people out. The weight of the words on that page had been heavier than anything I could've imagined. I walked into an appointment hoping for answers and came out being told there weren't any.

I had tried everything at that point to get rid of the chronic pain I was experiencing. I ruled everything out through blood tests upon blood tests and MRIs. I changed my diet, and at that point in time, I also seemed to take every supplement known to mankind. I had no idea why I was in so much pain, but on that day, the end didn't seem near.

Standing in that parking lot in downtown Redding, I was at a loss. My heart was heavy. My body was in pain. What now? Well. That morning I headed over to the building where the ministry school I was a part of had class every day. I worshipped and was surrounded by the community God so intentionally surrounded me with that year. Nobody but that doctor and my mom knew the latest.

The words of the world attempted to pull me under that day, but it was also that day that I "not so coincidentally" walked straight into my only option. Jesus.

I didn't have a plan B. He was the only One I knew who could provide for me what I needed at that point.

He was the only One that knew the root of my pain, the only One that could give me the wisdom for what to do and the only One who could show me how to make it through.

He was able to hold me, bringing a healing, heavenly comfort this world couldn't provide, while simultaneously promising to lead me out into a beautiful, broad place. He became the answer that day. He became the only option for me. It was Him all along and that day, I saw it clearly with my own eyes.

Jesus, Jesus, it would only ever be Jesus for me.

And what a beautiful option that was.

The healing hasn't manifested in my body yet, but Faithful and True is my God and I know that healing is His will. It isn't wishful thinking but rather standing on promises He has made and seeing Him as Jehovah Rapha not based on my circumstances but rather because that is who He says He is.

And right in the middle of it all, I choose to believe that. I choose to pursue Him, knowing that nothing else makes sense. Pursuing Him not for what He can do for me but for who He is.

All that He is, is all that I have searched this world for and have come up empty-handed by.

He is everything I desire and so much more.

It's Jesus.

My Provider, my Savior, my Deliverer, my Healer, my Song.

Since that day, I have come up against other people saying similar words that could create hopelessness if I held onto those words.

But as the world tells me one thing, I intentionally lean into God, who continues to whisper life-giving truth and the most beautiful reality of all.

"Choose me, and let Me be your option."

I can't write about why the healing hasn't come yet but I stand on what I do know. And that is the place that I choose to write from.

Jehovah Rapha and His faithfulness woven throughout this story He is writing...that is the story that I will tell, that is the song that I will sing.

As I write these words, I am reminded of this scripture:

"He's the hope that holds me and the Stronghold to shelter me, the only God for me, and my great confidence." (Psalm 91:2, TPT)

The world might look at a circumstance, diagnosis, or other pain and say, "losing options," but I have found that to be the very place I have encountered my God in a way I wouldn't have known Him otherwise.

I challenge you to do the same. In any situation where it seems impossible and you feel like you have hit a dead end, invite God in to be all that you need Him to be and more. He is ready, He is willing, He is so very near.

The dead end doesn't need to be the end.

Lean into Him and let it be the beginning of so much more that this world simply cannot be for us. Let Him be your refuge today.

"Wait for the Lord; be strong, and let your heart take courage; wait for the Lord." (Psalm 27:14, ESV)

Queue Treatment

A lot of life happened after I left the home in Sacramento. It was now 2024. Ten years after my first admission to this hospital, I was back. How did I get here? I remember fear taking hold of me that day as my therapist drove me to the hospital. I had a fear of sharing a room with a stranger, a fear of my privacy being stripped from me and, soon enough, my clothes too. They walked me back to the little padded room that had a camera perched in the corner, a bed, and a TV. It felt like the next few moments pushed me onto the floor, knocked the wind out of me, and reminded me that I had zero control at this point. A lady came in to search me. I remember crying telling her, "No, no, no." as a camera was in the room, and she couldn't have cared less but to come in and search me naked. I didn't feel like a human in that moment. That moment retraumatized me, playing through my head for weeks after. The only thing people could hear from the outside of that room was my crying. Wailing. Devastation. How did I end back up in this place? At this hospital. An EKG was barely done as I couldn't stay still or relax. Labs were drawn but even that was a blur to me. It happened and I don't remember when. I lay there curled up for hours. And soon enough, I was given a pair of matching forest green top and bottom. It was time to go upstairs. Escorted by a police officer, I landed on another floor, where they held me until a bed was available in the psychiatric unit.

I curled up on a bed in another holding room they had for me. Wrapping myself as tight as I could in a white blanket, I asked the nurse to turn the TV off as I stared outside for the next few hours. I watched as cars drove in and out, and people rushed across the crosswalk to their next destination, leaving their jobs for the day. A lady came in to hand me food, and I made no eye contact with her. She placed the food next to my bed. Another lady came in asking me to drink water, and with everything in me, I took a few sips of water.

Later in the evening there was yelling and screaming from a patient outside of my door. Shaken up but half asleep from medication, I walked in a circle around my room, wondering what to do, then got back in bed and tried to fall asleep. Around 1 am, I was woken up by two gentlemen saying it was time to go upstairs to the actual psych unit. Once again escorted by police, for the next hour, I sat upstairs as they went through my belongings. The next morning, I was frozen in fear. I hid behind a pole because of a man that was staring at me and I sat at a table, unable to eat any food. This continued for four days.

I felt like my body was becoming numb to life and alive to death. But in that dying, I was shaken awake. It was like lightning and thunder marked my seven days in the hospital. Wild, blinding flashes of lightning and rolling thunder shook me awake. My heart began to feel like it was waking up. Seven days completed my stay there. Completion. Stepping into more treatment was going to be just the beginning of a long journey ahead, but my heart was awake and I was beginning to hear His heartbeat again.

During my seven days spent in the hospital, I went into a meeting with my treatment team one morning, thinking we would be discussing a discharge date. Instead, the head doctor began to list off all that wasn't right with my body, my labs, and my EKG. Was he trying to scare me? Because it was working. He said, "Don't be surprised when they come up to get an x-ray of your heart this morning." How could this be so bad? My stomach dropped. Within thirty seconds, other doctors barged into the room, interrupted the meeting, and said, "We are ready for Annie." I felt like I was living in a nightmare. Everyone on the unit was aware of what was going on. Next thing I know, I am getting an X-ray done on my bed. Moments later, labs were drawn two more times because once at 7:20 am wasn't enough. Later that afternoon, I had five doctors approach me, asking me questions I only knew half of the answers to. I didn't know my body was in the state that it was in. But it was enough to wake me up and scare me in a good way. I didn't want to live like this. Things needed to change. I wanted something different. A life outside of this eating disorder. "I can't live like this anymore," I continued to think to myself.

A few days later, I told the treatment team, "I'm ready to live life differently. I am ready to take things seriously." It's not that I wasn't taking things seriously, but being half in is much different than being all in with recovery.

I was shaken awake in unforeseen, painful, scary circumstances, but my God is Emmanuel and El Roi. He is forever with me and sees me and will turn all things bitter into something so sweet. That's the story I get to tell, even in the middle of it all. Because that's where I am, hand in hand with Him.

Once I left the hospital, my treatment team had already made the decision that I needed a higher level of care. So continues the queue of treatment centers and admissions. One, two, three, four, five. Five treatment centers in 2024. If anyone needed a definition of treatment fatigue, I could most definitely have given it to them. I was simply exhausted. It felt like I was receiving the right help but being dragged along from one place to the next. I was tired of going through the motions of being in "treatment."

One of the treatment centers was up North so my mom and I made a road trip out of it. We've been on long cross-country road trips in the past, but this beat the record with us going from Raleigh to Chicago in one day. We finished the last part of the drive the next day. I had to go to the hospital to get medical clearance before arriving at the treatment center. I didn't know what to expect in this process. I knew I wasn't alone with the support I had from my family and close friends who knew about where I was but I still felt like I was doing it on my own in a way. But never alone and never on my own. My God was with me in that entire process. After a few hours were spent at that hospital, I was cleared to go over to the treatment center. I hugged my mom goodbye and I checked in. I was filling out paperwork when a lady came by and introduced herself. She was the one who would be putting a tracker on my wrist for the rest of the time that I was there. The tracker would tell the staff where I was at all times. There was no leaving that place "by accident" or intentionally. Not until they cut the band off on my discharge date.

After I dealt with that, I made my way to the inpatient unit with that lady and my big black suitcase. I walked in and all eyes were on me. I got searched and then talked with the medical provider while two other staff members went through my suitcase in a different room. Later that afternoon, I was talking with one of the nurses about how I loved to write but ironically, the desk had been taken out of my room for safety reasons with a previous patient. She put in an order for a desk to be put back in, and before I went to sleep that night, I was lying next to a desk on the right side of my bed! I saw God in the details of that. He cares about the littlest things.

My time there wasn't easy. I called someone from home every day on the phones they gave us access to at certain times of the day. I felt that being closer to home would be good for me during treatment and so the next place I was referred to was back in North Carolina.

To the Girl in Room 205

To the girl in room 205,
you're going to be okay. You didn't sign up for this. I know you're scared. I know you feel alone. I know you don't feel as if you are being heard, understood, or cared for. The ache you feel, the confusion you feel. It is immeasurable.

You walk out of that room and put a smile on your face. You are a friend to everyone simply because you know what it's like not to have one. You see the one person who is sitting alone and you send them a little smile across the hall, across the room, just so they feel seen. You know what it's like not to be.

You sit out on the bench waiting for your meds. You wait, you wait, you wait some more. The day has already started. It's 7:10 a.m. and the nurses are in the midst of their shift change. They make it known with the note they just put on the med window. "Meds at 7:30." You wonder who is going to be working that day. Rumor has it that X and X are working. It's either a sigh or a relief. One or the other. Some make you feel seen and heard. Others do the opposite. It's a strange thing how we all want to be heard, understood, and loved. We are all searching for it. But only some can give it in that setting. Maybe it's just a bad day. Maybe they never knew it themselves.

But to the girl in room 205,

you're right in the middle of your hardest battle. And what if I told you that this would be worth it? What if I told you that this battle would be fought and won? That you would make it through. That you would one day be on the other side of this. One breath. One step. One meal. One therapy session. One snack with your dietician. One walk down the hallway and session with the psychiatrist at a time. You're doing it. You're doing the hard things you never thought you could do. The things you never wanted to do. You're winning. Just by being. You hear a strong and strengthening whisper to your heart, "Be still and know."

What if I told you that you could rest in a peace that surpassed all understanding because the Prince of Peace understands what you're going through? He knows exactly what you need to get through all that you are going through. He knows in the purest sense. He knows. The only one that carries the ability to withhold omniscience — we get to give our lives over to Him. What a beautiful thing. A beautiful reality.

To the girl in room 205, you are scared. You stand on the inside of your bedroom door, just waiting for the courage to walk outside to meet the people that await you on the other side. You stand there just wondering what you will have to tend to on the other side. What conversations will take place? You carry a fear for what will take place on the other side of the door. You pace the backside of the hallway until you know you will eventually be told to stop. But you keep going. You think to yourself, "They just don't understand." Once again, feeling misunderstood.

It's time to go to the meal room. You knew going into this it would be a lot. You've been through this before. But for someone whose strength is spent, six times in the meal room a day feels absolutely impossible. Exhaustion woven through your body, your mind, your words, and your thoughts. You do it day in and day out.

You sit at the table with five others but in a room full of others. You're monitored. They watch you eat. They serve you Kate Farms (dairy-free version of Boost) if you don't finish. You wonder how things got to this point. You begin to feel the anger from within rise as you think of the memories and the people that have led you to this very place. The root issues. The root pain. Was it all just you? Or was it all him? Was it both? But on the surface, you're simply pouring granola into some dairy-free yogurt and slowly eating it as you watch the clock. You're cutting (or tearing it if you can't yet use a knife) your sandwich into fours and told not to by staff sitting at the table across from you. They're simply trying to help but it's a moment when helping hurts. I push my plate away. How could this be? Doing your best, but your best isn't good enough. Criticized for doing your best. You didn't finish your meal. Kate Farms, it'll be. To the girl in room 205, I am sorry.

Some days in the meal room, you would tune out all of the loud noise until it was just you and the plate of food in front of you. It helped you get through the meal. I am proud of you.

Some days, you were so in tune with the noises that surrounded you that it was empowering the littlest of fear until you had to leave the room — which, of course, isn't even allowed. But you found a way. You always found a way. I am still proud of you.

Somedays, you engaged in conversation, laughed, asked questions, and it took all of you. I am so proud of you.

You found a haven in that room of yours — room 205. God met you there. Well, you met Him. You felt like He was already waiting for you whenever you retreated. Ran. Hid. You hid but He would whisper, "I am here. Even in your hiding. And when you're ready, I'll be with you...to come out of hiding. Hand in hand, to come out of hiding."

Whether your therapist found you, the yoga therapist, or a nurse, you were always always always first met by God. How faithful. How true. Always good, isn't He?

You saw some of the darkest hours at night in that room. Room 205. You felt unheard and misunderstood. Not by clinicians (if anything, you have never felt more advocated for than by your team when you were in treatment residing in that room) but by others that you came across.

That room created space for you to encounter your God in a way that you wouldn't have if it weren't for those difficult encounters at night. If it weren't for those certain conversations. If it weren't for those confusing moments of not feeling like you were being treated like a human. Feeling like a number. One, two, three, how pitiful. Oh, we live in a fallen world. Living with an eating disorder didn't make things easier. It made you more vulnerable. That room saw the worst of it. But you also were able to create a haven there. Because, well, God was there.

To the girl in room 205,

You are safe.

You are seen.

You are heard. You have a voice.

You are understood.

Continue to advocate for yourself because in doing so you are paving a way for others to also be heard and understood.

To the girl in room 205, I am sorry for not giving you enough grace during those darkest of nights. You are me. And you got through some of the darkest, hardest of days. Refining. God is refining. These days are defining. These days are marking. There's a story being told. It's unfolding before our eyes. Being in room 205 was just a glimpse of that. Just a glimpse.

This will all be a part of a story one day.

It opened our eyes to how things shouldn't be and how things should be. It opened our eyes to how faithful our God is. It opened our eyes to the kindest of therapists and the best trauma-informed yoga therapist. To wildly sweet and funny nurses. To the best of psychiatrists who advocate for and educate, not just medicate. It opened our eyes to how small this world is and how big our God is. He was in the details of you... me... being in room 205. Without a doubt. Although at times it felt like I didn't have a voice, using my voice found my way into that room.

Keep fighting. One day. One hour. One step. One meal. One breath. One conversation at a time. Keep advocating for yourself. You've got this.

And to all who reside in room 205 after me. God is so willing and able to meet you in that place. This I know. I met Him there myself. He is waiting. You are not alone.

To the One Struggling to Find Hope

Hold on. This isn't the end. I know it might feel like it. I haven't been in your exact situation but I have been in a place where hope was stripped from me. Where I felt I had no purpose, no reason, and no motivation. I've been in places where I questioned if life is worth living, and I've been in places where I have declared life is not worth living and taken action. I've sat on the bathroom floor night after night, unable to see a light at the end. I have been worn out and exhausted and simply just done. "What's the purpose of anything anymore?"

It would be nice to have a specific formula to lay out and say, "Here you go!" "Here's the answer." I, for one, never thought I would see the light. I never thought I would have hope for tomorrow. I never thought I would have the strength to take another step forward. But God has given me strength, and now there are days when I am dancing my way forward. This one thing I can point you towards in your darkest of moments, and that is our Jesus. He is patient, kind, and faithful. Be reminded that you are never alone in your battles. Be reminded that depression is not your destiny. There's more life for you to live. To be able to tap into the joy of the

Lord and not just experience it for yourself but to be able to release it to others. Hold on. Keep holding. When your arms get tired, fall into your Father's arms. Hope is alive.

His Words that Sustained Me

"One thing have I asked of the Lord, that will I seek after: that I may dwell in the house of the Lord all the days of my life, to gaze upon the beauty of the Lord and to inquire in his temple." (Psalm 27:4, ESV)

This one thing have I asked of the Lord, and this one thing have I clung to. To dwell in the house of the Lord all the days of my life and to gaze upon His beauty. There is no one like Him. Not one. Nobody and nothing else satisfies.

"He who dwells in the shelter of the Most High will abide in the shadow of the Almighty. I will say to the LORD, "My refuge and my fortress, my God, in whom I trust." For he will deliver you from the snare of the fowler and from the deadly pestilence. He will cover you with his pinions, and under his wings you will find refuge; his faithfulness is a shield and buckler. You will not fear the terror of the night, nor the arrow that flies by day, nor the pestilence that stalks in darkness, nor the destruction that wastes at noonday. A thousand may fall at your side, ten thousand at your right hand, but it will not come near you. You will only look with your eyes and see the recompense of the wicked. Because you have made the LORD your dwelling place — the Most High, who is my refuge — no evil shall be allowed to befall you, no plague come near your tent. For he will command his angels concerning you to guard you in all your ways. On their hands they will bear you up, lest you strike your foot against a stone. You will tread on the lion and the adder; the young lion and the serpent you will trample underfoot. "Because he holds fast to me in love, I will deliver him; I will protect him, because he knows my name. When he calls to me, I will answer him; I will be with him in trouble; I will rescue him and honor him. With long life I will satisfy him and show him my salvation." (Psalm 91:1-16, ESV)

I remember the day I read this psalm for the first time. I was at my mentor's house and she pulled out a piece of paper that had Psalm 91 written on it. She told me it was a scripture that she held fast to in times when she felt anxiety and thought I could do the same. Later that year I memorized the Psalm. To have it replaying in my head constantly felt like a weapon in my hand and my mind to use against the enemy. I was protected. I had a dwelling place. The Lord was my refuge. With Him near, I didn't have to fear. I was safe.

"And we know that for those who love God all things work together for good, for those who are called according to his purpose." (Romans 8:28, ESV)

This scripture encouraged me when I wasn't so sure all things in my life could be used by God. I went through a season where I thought that ten years of my life were wasted and stolen from me. But this passage says that every detail is woven together for good, not one thing missing.

"May the God of hope fill you with all joy and peace as you trust in him, so that you may overflow with hope by the power of the Holy Spirit" (Romans 15:13, ESV)

"Or do you not know that your body is a temple of the Holy Spirit within you, whom you have from God? You are not your own," (1 Corinthians 6:19, ESV)

"But we have this treasure in jars of clay, to show that the surpassing power belongs to God and not to us. We are afflicted in every way, but not crushed; perplexed, but not driven to despair; persecuted, but not forsaken; struck down, but not destroyed; always carrying in the body the death of Jesus, so that the life of Jesus may also be manifested in our bodies." (2 Corinthians 4:7-10, ESV)

"so that by two unchangeable things, in which it is impossible for God to lie, we who have fled for refuge might have strong encouragement to hold fast to the hope set before us. We have this as a sure and steadfast anchor of the soul, a hope that enters into the inner place behind the curtain, where Jesus has gone as a forerunner on our behalf, having become a high priest forever after the order of Melchizedek." (Hebrews 6:18-20, ESV)

Jesus Christ is the same yesterday and today and forever. (Hebrews 13:8, ESV)

To the One Alone on the Bathroom Floor

I have been where you are. It's lonely. It can get scary. It can be confusing. You probably are weary and exhausted. You feel everything but understood right now. You might feel forgotten about or feel like nobody cares. But if there is one thing I could tell you right now it would be your strength comes from the Lord. Don't give up just yet. There's hope. Feeling the cold tile of the bathroom floor and physically feeling your chest ache from the pain you're in feels never-ending. You just want it to end. And it will. It won't last forever. Whether there are others on the other side of the door trying to get your attention or if the house is completely empty with not a sound to be heard, the enemy is still fighting for your attention. Try for one moment to forget about him and what he is having you focus on. Ask the Lord to show you a glimmer of hope. Ask Him to show up in the details of your life. Ask Him to reveal Himself and His tangible presence to you. He loves you. He sees you. He has not abandoned you. He hears your cry. His heart is to bring healing. Restoration. Whether it's to your heart, your mind, or your family. Invite God in. Allow Him to be at the center. Let the Holy Spirit be your comforter. You are not alone. In Matthew 11:28-30, Jesus says,

"Come to me, all who labor and are heavy laden, and I will give you rest. Take my yoke upon you, and learn from me, for I am gentle and lowly in heart, and you will find rest for your souls. For my yoke is easy, and my burden is light." And know that Emmanuel is in this moment.

To the Girl Wondering if
Freedom is Possible

The doctors tell you that they wish they had a magic wand to help you. You're left to wonder if it'll always be this way. You sit in treatment centers and hear dry words that carry death and can suck the life and hope out of someone, "You'll always struggle to some extent." You hear that you're always at a higher than average risk for suicide because of treatment-resistant depression. You keep being referred from one therapist to the next because nobody knows how to help you. You wonder if you'll ever become unstuck and find freedom. Does any of this sound familiar? Well, I know I have been in this place, and I have felt these things, and I know I can't be alone in it. If that's you, know this: freedom is available. The invitation to come to Jesus is always available. He is the only one who can be called Savior, Deliverer, and Healer. He desires to be that for us. Next time you hear words about your future that don't carry hope, know that it isn't the Lord. Jeremiah 29:11 says, "For I know the plans I have for you, declares the LORD, plans for welfare and not for evil, to give you a future and a hope." We get to cling to that Truth as believers. How beautiful. Your life isn't meant to be lived in a cage of labels and diagnoses. Don't let them reign over your life. God speaks a better word.

Choose Life, Not Death

Journal Entry: No more taking my life from Him. Deuteronomy 30:19 says, "I call heaven and earth to witness against you today, that I have set before you life and death, blessing and curse. Therefore choose life, that you and your offspring may live." Proverbs 18:21 says, "Death and life are in the power of the tongue." The least I can do is give Him my life again and again and again and again. No more trying to take my life. He can have it all. He wants it all and He can have it all. Somehow, in the ways I have hated myself, hated my life, wanting to take my life and throw away my life and discard it, I am loving my life more than I am loving Him. I am loving the opinions of man more than I am loving the Lord and what He thinks. Wow. Loving man more than God. How can that be? He gave His life to save mine. The least I could do is let Him lead mine, be in mine, have a say, and take up space, all the space. Today, I choose LIFE. I speak LIFE. Will you?

Freedom Found in Surrender

The Lord gave me a vision one day of someone being rescued by a lifeguard. At first, the person began trying to fight on their own, and the more they did that, the closer they were to drowning. It was doing them no good. They became more worn out and exhausted. In the next scene, the person was yielding to the lifeguard. Choosing to yield. Surrendering. Not fighting it. Fighting it would only make things worse. The lifeguard has your best in mind. They have your life in mind. They see from a perspective you can't see from. In a similar way, it's like when a baby is in need of something, crying and trying to wiggle out of the father's arms. The father knows exactly what that baby's needs are, and it does more harm to let the baby wiggle out than to hold them tight and suit their needs. Our Savior asks us to yield and surrender to Him. It's in that surrender, that we are able to find freedom. It's in the letting go of worldly things that we have room to hold hands with the King of Kings. It's in the laying down that we clear the clutter enough to gaze upon the beauty of the Lord. How much more does Jesus have your best in mind over a lifeguard? You can trust your life with Jesus!

Even in the Waiting

God's promises are true even in the waiting — promises backed by the beauty of His faithfulness.

Holding tight to His sweet whispers of wisdom and revelation. Whispers filled with mystery that draw me in, fill me with wonder, and open my eyes to the reality that there is so much more that I have yet to discover or see.

Whispers that draw me close. Warm, tender, strong whispers — "It's okay to let the walls down."

Words wrapped in a sense of trust. Knowing that what He says is pure and true. Words that allow me to let down the walls I have built up in order to protect.

Coming under the canopy of Love, He becomes my Protector, He becomes my Comforter. I feel seen — but this time, I've never felt so safe. Whispers of love that carry the power to drown all fear. Whispers of light — life-giving light that the darkness cannot extinguish. Whispers of life that make a heart come alive — awakening hope, dreams, and purpose.

Whispers of healing that say no heart is too broken that it can't be made whole.

His whispers — I have never known something so tender and comforting yet so full of authority and power. The lion of the tribe of Judah — on my side. Fighting with and for me.

Even as I am in the waiting.

I'm learning the beauty of seeking and finding.

Of learning.

Of growing.

Of blooming. Nothing can hinder growth when I am rooted in Love.

Nothing can stand against.

The waiting — not a place where I am making my home, but knowing there is something so beautiful to be found here in this place all the while.

God, open my eyes to see you in the waiting. Bring peace to my heart to not fight this place but rather keep my eyes on you and find you here in the midst of this. I pray for everyone else reading these words today. I pray that you will reveal yourself to them in a new way today. Come close and reveal yourself as Emmanuel. Near. Bringing divine insight, wisdom, and revelation. I pray that the places that have seemed dry, where people have felt weary and wondered how much longer they will have to wait to see a breakthrough or a new season, I pray that you will infuse them with your strength, enveloping them in your love and your presence. Fill us with overwhelming joy and peace — even in the waiting!

His Presence in the Pain

Knowing His presence even in the midst of pain.
Knowing His presence, closer than the pain.
This has been something that I have challenged myself to become aware of.
Not trying hard to find something that doesn't feel possible to grab hold of, but rather become aware of what is already present — His presence. Here with me now. Even in the pain.

In 2018, I moved to northern California to attend a ministry school. I would walk every morning from my apartment over to where I had classes. During that short ten-minute walk, I always felt the Lord come close and encourage me. One morning I heard the Holy Spirit say that the season I was in would be one marked by His presence and known for that rather than the pain that seemed so persistent at the time. Persistent was the pain, but so powerful and present was His presence.

During these moments where pain can be so easy to get lost in, I have been reminded of those words and that truth.

Pain within my body seems too close at times. Unable to get out of it or escape it. But there is a greater reality I can get lost in. Not one of numbing pain but a reality where I become so aware of His presence. The Prince of Peace is closer still.

I don't have to fear when He is near.

I don't have to be anxious about the pain when His presence, within me and all around me, gives me peace. He introduces me to a pure, heavenly peace that surpasses my understanding. I lean in close to the one acquainted with suffering Himself. I feel understood, seen, and strengthened. His presence is a promise I cling to.

Mbale, Uganda

J ournal entry: The other morning, I woke up, walked out of the room I was staying in, and looked out at the life slowly awakening in the city of Mbale, Uganda. I was hit with an overwhelming sense of thankfulness for being alive. I stood there, not wanting to leave the moment I had found myself in. Fully aware of the wrap-around presence of my God — the one who loves to tangibly reveal Himself to us. Standing there letting Him love on me, I remember thinking that I wouldn't forget that moment. Life — something that a few years ago I thought I didn't want to be a part of — believing the lie that I didn't have a part to play. But oh, when God breathes on dry bones. There has been a fresh awakening. Opening my eyes to see that I was born into a living hope. A living, unshakable hope. Life was something I was meant to be a part of — pulling Heaven down to earth — to be a walking encounter of God's love, His joy, His hope, His peace.

What a wonderful feeling to be alive in that moment, that morning in Mbale.

His breath was in my lungs. My heart, beating — beating to the rhythm of Heaven. Beating to the rhythm of perfect love — love that leaves no room for fear.

Caught up in His presence — I had locked eyes with a Love more beautiful than life itself. A Love that stirs up dreams, purpose, passion, and vision. A Love that has made me come alive. Awakening me to the reality that God always desired for me to live in. The reality that I am meant to live in. The reality that I am meant to tell of.

I'll never forget that moment.

Standing in the stillness and quiet — overwhelmed by the grace of my Heavenly Father who never stopped pursuing me, always protected me and directed my steps to that very place in Mbale, Uganda. Opening my eyes to this incredible gift called life.

He met me there that morning, encountering my heart and making me so aware of His nearness — His breath in my lungs. His breath that has made me come alive. Fully alive.

Annie, You're Okay. Just Look at Me.

There is so much power in one glance at our Savior.

"Annie, you're okay. Just look at Me."

God spoke these words at a Sunday evening church service a few years ago.

In between worship and the message that night, there were some students who were hearing words of encouragement from God about certain people and ministering to those of us in the room.

One of the students heard lyrics to the Michael Jackson song titled "Smooth Criminal." The lyrics repeat over and over: "Annie, are you okay?".

She then went on to say that there were people in the room who were experiencing the enemy coming in like a smooth criminal with the question "Are you okay?" making us question how we really are doing.

During the months leading up to this night, I had been in the throes of much confusion, pain, and exhaustion surrounding my health. Determined to get chronic pain under control, more Friday mornings than not, I would have an appointment with my doctor in search of finding relief.

During these months I also was constantly questioning if I was okay. Questioned by myself or by others — those words shifted my focus onto my circumstances and what I was feeling. My eyes noticed everything that felt misaligned, everything that looked as if it was up in flames.

But that Sunday evening, God spoke through this student, saying, "Annie, you're okay. Just look at Me. You're going to be okay." I knew He was speaking directly into my situation. And how much more personal could He get than calling out my name?

He wasn't dismissing my pain. He wasn't dismissing my health or the confusion I felt. But He did have an answer that this world couldn't provide for me. He had the hope I had been searching for. He was the hope I had been searching for. He wanted to bring me up a little higher that night to see things from His perspective. He wanted me to know I was okay and that He was right there in the middle of it with me. He said, "Look at Me. You're okay. Keep your eyes on Me."

The Lord recently reminded me of this word that was spoken. It was a reminder I needed for the moment I am in, but I feel like He is saying the same thing right now to anyone who feels bound by fear, anxiety, or any situation that seems hopeless.

He isn't dismissing the issue that's causing you to feel that way. He isn't denying that the root of your fear, worry, and anxiety is something very real. But He is wanting you to come up a little higher.

To see things from His perspective. To see and to know a better reality. A reality that carries peace, hope, life, freedom, and healing.

Hear Him speak into your situation: "You're going to be ok. Just look at Me." Find Him in the midst of this. He's here right in the middle of whatever it is that you're walking through. He has the answer you're looking for. It's Him. He's closer than you think.

Find His eyes. Look into His eyes and ask Him what He's saying to you in this moment. His eyes are full of love. Full of grace. Full of promises. Full of the strength you need to take one step in front of the other. Looking into His eyes, you'll find His eyes have been on you all along. Looking into His eyes, you'll find that that's exactly where you belong. I promise you'll find all that you need in this moment.

He's glorious.

He's beautiful.

He's so, so very personal.

"You're okay. Just look at Me."

To the Girl Feeling Pain For The First Time

Hold onto His nail-pierced hands, and don't let go.
Hands that know suffering. He knows suffering.
He's well acquainted with it himself.
Gaze into His eyes.
He may speak no words.
But even in silence, you will feel understood by Him.
Acknowledged, seen, understood. You'll try to feel understood by others. Being misunderstood has become one of your biggest fears. You seek understanding from all. But seek Him. Only He truly understands the pain.

You'll come to know that His presence is all you need, and it will carry you through. It'll carry you through when medication doesn't. It'll carry you through when words from family and friends can't. It'll carry you through when blood tests, X-rays, and ultrasounds detect nothing. It'll carry you through when doctors have no answers but a label.

His presence is everything. Hold His hands — hands full of understanding, suffering, victory, healing — and don't let go. Gaze into the eyes that don't dismiss your pain, and don't lose sight of Him. He understands. Oh, and He heals. He is Healer.

Don't search the world for what He already has for you — sweet, abundant healing. "Wait for the Lord; be strong, and let your heart take courage; wait for the Lord." (Psalm 27:14, ESV)

Your story will be one of Him turning bitter into sweet, for He is Jehovah Rapha. Hold onto His nail-pierced hands, and don't let go. Hold onto hope, for your healing is on the horizon.

To the girl seven years ago feeling chronic pain for the first time, you're going to be okay.

Simply Annie With a
New Diagnosis

Monday, February 10th, 2025. It was just like any other Monday morning. I had an appointment at eleven o'clock and I came home. Well, besides that, nothing about this day was normal. I had another appointment at two o'clock that afternoon that I had to get home for. The lady on the other side of the screeen would be waiting for me. I had waited almost two months for the two appointments that I had with her and this was going to be the last of them. Today, she was going to give me a diagnosis. I waited on the other side of the screen for ten minutes until she came on. I somehow arrived early. That was the only part of the day that I was anxious about — possibly being late for the appointment. I sat in my chair, curled up with a blanket, placing my hands back and forth along the white paint of my desk, waiting for her arrival.

She started the meeting and we began where we had left off. Talking about autism. I already knew the direction this last meeting would be going in based on the previous appointment, tests we went over, and a conversation I had had with my therapist.

I wasn't anxious. I wasn't excited. I was simply at peace.

For me, to open up to a stranger is hard but for every question she asked me, I felt I could be completely honest with her. She created such a safe space.

After a few hours of tests, appointments, and months of waiting, she told me that I had autism.

Her words didn't scare me. Her words also didn't surprise me. It was almost like the more she talked, the more she was giving me permission to be myself.

Over the last couple of months I have only started to process what this means for me.

To begin with, why tell the world? Well. What is there to hide? I haven't changed. I'm the same me that I was before I had the diagnosis. What is there to be ashamed of?

I'm also a writer. I process a lot of things through writing and this has been one of those things. It's not a surprise to me that I've shared some of my journey of getting this diagnosis either because I have always been about people feeling less alone in their own journey.

I have only begun to grasp what this means and has meant for me. There were years when elementary school Annie struggled, but other labels were attached carelessly. So much of my elementary and middle school years start to make sense when I look at them with this new diagnosis in mind. In high school, I was misdiagnosed with a personality disorder when really I was autistic. It makes me sad, but it also gives me so much clarity and closure for those years.

What now? Nothing new. I am the same me. Still choosing to be simply Annie over here. But there's more learning and more awareness to come. From the beginning, I have felt as if I have had a dictionary in one hand learning all there is to know and a pen in the other hand processing and writing about all that now makes sense to me from years past. More words will spill from my heart soon and land on these platforms as it is all still new to me. Read my words at www.anniesnyder.com as well as on my social media @anniesnyd to stay up to date on this new journey that I am on.

Former Therapists,
Forever Thankful.

I couldn't just write one general letter to everyone because my time with each of you has been so unique. I appreciate you all so much and wouldn't be where I am today without your support. I've been so blessed with each of you being my therapists over the years. Like, really blessed. Thank you.

Rebecca, I've known you for eleven years, and although you haven't always been my therapist during those years, I've always been thankful that our paths have crossed. I met you when I was eighteen. I was depressed, anxious, and had absolutely no desire to live. Throughout the years, you've shown me a whole lot of compassion. You've shown me a ton of grace. You've met me where I was at. You've always spoken the truth, even if it was hard for me to hear. You challenged me, pushed me, and always cheered me on when I did exposures. I never felt alone when you were my therapist. I knew you were right alongside me, fighting with me. You saw me through hospital visits, treatment centers, my "Annie in Africa" days, and so much more. When I came back to you at twenty-nine, you were the first one that asked me if I had ever considered being on the spectrum, and it changed everything for me. I am so thankful for you!

Dear RM, 2015 Annie would sit on the couch in your office, stare at the ground, and say, "I don't know" ...a lot. There was shame to my story. I was wrapped in it. Every word was driven by it. But you consistently showed up for me. Both before I left for treatment in Georgia and Florida and when I came back. Even when I was struggling in Atlanta, you made time for emails and phone calls. You always fit me into your schedule. Multiple times a week. It was needed for sure, but it also meant a lot to me. You were always happy to see me and never failed to show me my way out of that maze of a building. You understood that the easiest way I communicated was through writing and always welcomed me to write my thoughts out in emails to you. You made space for me to feel heard and seen. You never made me feel like a burden. I'm pretty sure you received hundreds of those emails. Thank you, and I'm sorry. I appreciated the peace you carried and the compassion you had. You always made me feel welcome and less alone. I looked forward to my appointments with you, even on the hardest of days. You were the first person I opened up to about my OCD struggles — years after it began. You educated me and were never judgmental. You were safe. Your office was safe. Thank you for everything. I'll always be thankful that our paths crossed.

Cat, it was my first day in a residential treatment facility when I was walking down the hall and saw you. I passed by your office, and you said, "Are you Annie?! I'm going to be your therapist." In our first meeting, you noticed that I had written Psalm 91 down on my hand, and you made reference to it. I knew I was in the right office. I received an email at one point in my journey there saying, "Just thinking of you and praying over you now. You are doing such good work...You can do this. God will give you the strength. You are His beloved; you are good enough." Another encouraging email: "I will fight the enemy alongside you. You have so much you can do to redeem creation and love those whom others forget. What a beautiful heart God has given you." Cat, you sat with me as I was curled up in the office chair next to your desk, with my colorful Guatemala blanket wrapped around me. You were the first person to tell me I had an eating disorder. You gave me an answer and a name to what was going on. You sat there with me as we called my parents to tell them. You saw me through my transition to the eating disorder facility in Florida, and although I felt disappointed, not once did I feel like you were giving up on me. Also, remember that time you treated me to a Starbucks trip? It's the little things that meant a lot. I really appreciate you and all of your prayers.

TR, a word that marked my sessions with you would be "vision". I remember one day when I was having such intense anxiety. The treatment team was unsure whether or not I needed to be sent elsewhere. You sat in the back room with me that day and let me skip group. We talked about previous mission trips I had been on, and we talked about future ones I would go on. You made space for me to dream. In the midst of the pain and chaos, you helped me see that there's a life outside of the eating disorder and that things will get better someday. I would hear in treatment that I'd always struggle to some extent, but when I talked to you, there was always hope attached. You reminded me of the truth. You supported my writing and were always the first to read a blog post. You reminded me daily to give myself grace. I'm thankful that my recovery journey landed me in Atlanta, not only because I discovered lavender lattes but also because you were my therapist. Thanks for everything!

Kathleen, wow, where do I even begin?! You saw me through so much. You met me where I was at. You showed me what it was like for a therapist to never give up on me. You carry so much peace, and as anxiety-ridden as that season was, I felt so much peace with you in that room. God was present there. You made space for Him. You welcomed Him into conversations, and we never forgot to talk about Him. I saw some dark, hopeless days during my time with you. I felt enveloped by the pain in my body. It weighed me down and stripped all strength from me. But you never gave up on me. Even when you didn't know what to do, you kept your door open for me. I've never known a therapist who would go as far as you did to learn what you've learned in order to try to help me. You educated me and taught me about how trauma stays stuck in the body. I'm thankful for every session we had, even the ones where it felt like we were getting nowhere. I know we both know that God used all of it for good, and He wastes nothing. Really, really thankful for you.

MJ, "Six to nine months at this residential home", I told everyone back home. But I somehow ended up being there for two weeks short of a year. I wouldn't change any of it because I had the best therapist. From my very first session with you to my last, I saw God in the details. You taught me to worship in the midst of pain and confusion. Let my life be worship! You showed me the importance of communion. The importance of the cross! The importance of the blood of the Lamb! Only by the blood was I able to forgive the man who abused me. Only by the blood was I able to forgive others in my life — still feeling the effects of forgiveness to this day. I'm so thankful you were by my side in that. You reminded me to look to the cross. It was there that I found strength from within. You were there when I said goodbye to Escape. It was you who challenged me to dream again and led me to the prayer room in the afternoons. It was with you that I had the revelation that Jesus didn't need the world to know what they had done in order for forgiveness to flow from His heart. He didn't need the world to understand. That session marked me for life. The "Choosing to Forgive" key marked me. I'm thankful you led me through that. It was with you that I found my voice both for seventh-grade Annie and for who I am now. It was with you that we sat in my car, prayed over it, and took communion. The past is in the past — another really powerful moment I experienced there at that home. I never felt judged by you. I only felt loved. Seen. Celebrated. I could go on and on. Wildly thankful for you.

Mariah! Residential treatment is no fun but you always made it easier. I was ashamed and wrapped in anxiety on that first day (of my first admission), but you made me feel so welcomed. You showed me to my room, you introduced me to others, and you had a big smile on your face. You made me feel like it wasn't the end of the world to be there. I would be alright. The word that marks my time with you would be "Celebrated". You knew how to celebrate the little things and the big things. I felt celebrated as a person by you. Just by seeing you in the hallway, you were happy to see me. On the day of my second admission there, you were working at a different location, but you came by just to say hi and give me a hug! It was the little things that were big. They were noticed. And I still find myself thankful. You have a heart for justice, and when somethings off, you make it right. Thank you for the times when you made things right for me. Also, remember that time we ate sloppy joes as a challenge? I was dreading it but somehow you and my dietician made it fun. Thankful for you.

Lauren, one of the hardest, most challenging things I did in my eating disorder recovery journey was with you! Well, it happened twice, and both times you helped give me the courage to do it. Although there were tears, somehow there were also laughs. I said goodbye to something that I haven't looked back at. I am so thankful for the safe space you created. I'm thankful that you always made a way for me to feel like I was getting support. If you saw me in the hallway, you found the way to sit there on the bench with me — even if it meant bringing your laptop out with you. I was always thankful for what you said to me, even if it was hard to hear. "Lauren said so" became a thing. I still think about things you've told me — especially "Give yourself grace, but don't give your eating disorder grace." Thank you for always making me feel heard and understood. Thankful for you, Lauren!

And L, I am most definitely making space for words I have written to you here as much as your title is not "therapist". You've played a vital role in my recovery for at least seven years. There have been seasons where I went months without seeing you, and there have been seasons where I have seen you weekly. In all of it, I have felt your support. You've seen me in some of my highest moments and you've met me in my lowest. You've seen the worst of me. You're safe. You're easy to talk to and tell things to. There have been moments when I was not in a good headspace, and you just knew. You met me where I was at. I've never felt ashamed talking with you. You saw me through my move to California, where I was in remission and doing so well. You saw me through that hospital visit and sat on the phone with the doctors there for more hours than you probably should've. You've seen me through my autism diagnosis. You take time to remind me of why I should choose recovery and simply take the time to listen and care. You remind me that I have one body to take care of. You recently told me that I was strong but not healthy and it changed everything for me. Anorexia has shown it's face to you. So has self-harm. So has SI and hospital visits. Along with terrible, stubborn phosphorus results. But you've never given up on me. You keep supporting me. I could go on and on. I wish everyone could have support like you in their life. You're intentional, thoughtful, caring — and just really good at your job. Thankful for you!

Do You Want a
Relationship With Jesus?

I f you've been reading through these chapters and hearing stories
about God being present but don't know if you have a relationship with Him, there's good news. There's always an invitation to
"come away" with Him. To choose Him. To say "yes" with all your
heart to Him. He's ready, waiting, with arms wide open. You were
the joy set before Him on the cross when He paid for your sins. Pray
this with me!

God, I need you! I can't do this without you. I need a Savior.
Helper. Comforter. The things of this world don't satisfy. I look to
you. I choose you today. I repent of my sins, surrender my life to you,
and I don't look back. My eyes are on you. I believe that Jesus is the
way, the truth, and the life. I believe that Jesus died on the cross for
my sins, and it's only by the blood of the Lamb that I can come close
and have a relationship with you. It's only by the blood that I can
see redemption, healing, hope, and the promise of peace in my life. I
make space for you today. Come and fill me with your Holy Spirit.
Make yourself known to me today in a way I have never known you.
I long to know you, Lord! In Jesus' name, Amen.

Hope

In the midst of treatment centers, bathroom floors, trying to take my life, and battling addiction, hope was always there. Hope was never lost. Hope was always alive. Sometimes just a little hidden from my sight in the storm. There, just unrecognizable. But the more I gazed upon the beauty of the Lord, the more I saw that hope was always there. Emmanuel was always with me. Faithful and True. I pray that as you have read through these pages and connected with different words or stories, that you will realize the same is true for you. You have a God who is Jehovah Rapha, El Roi, Emmanuel. A God who loves to show up in the littlest of details. Emmanuel in all our moments.

www.ingramcontent.com/pod-product-compliance
Lightning Source LLC
Chambersburg PA
CBHW031413120626

46545CB00006B/2128